remote luxury

top resorts down under

remote luxury

top resorts down under

Editor
Sabina Marreiros

Photography
Markus Bachmann

Text
Janelle McCulloch

images
Publishing

Published in Australia in 2007 by
The Images Publishing Group Pty Ltd
ABN 89 059 734 431
6 Bastow Place, Mulgrave, Victoria 3170, Australia
Tel: +61 3 9561 5544 Fax: +61 3 9561 4860
books@imagespublishing.com
www.imagespublishing.com

National Library of Australia Cataloguing-in-Publication entry:

Remote Luxury – Top resorts down under.

ISBN 9781864701982 (hbk.).

1. Resort architecture – Australia. 2. Resorts – Australia Design and construction.
3. Hotels – Australia – Design and construction. 4. Architecture and recreation – Australia.
5. Landscape – Australia – Design and construction.
I. Marreiros, Sabina. II. McCulloch, Janelle.

728.50994

Edited by Sabina Marreiros

Designed by The Graphic Image Studio Pty Ltd, Mulgrave, Australia
www.tgis.com.au

Digital production by Splitting Image Colour Studio Pty Ltd, Australia
Printed by Paramount Printing Company Limited Hong Kong

IMAGES has included on its website a page for special notices in relation to this and our other publications. Please visit www.imagespublishing.com.

Contents

Out of the blue...

Islands. They're the epitome of barefoot luxury. In fact, the very word connotes slow pleasures and remote bliss, far from the excess, pressure and stress of modern life. Think of an island and you think of empty beaches, pristine forests, languid lifestyles and a loss of time – the latter being as much of an attraction as the space, simplicity and silence. Indeed, such is the appeal of islands and other far-flung escapes in this fast-paced world that they have become the cool new places to get away. They are, quite simply, one of the best antidotes to modern life.

Two of the world's most beautiful islands are Australia and New Zealand. Famous for their scale, grand landscapes and natural beauty, so distinct from anything else in either the northern or southern hemispheres, they are now fashioning a reputation for innovative retreats that not only respect these sensitive landscapes and set an architectural precedent, but also offer a whole new, utterly mesmerizing style of laid-back luxury.

In New Zealand, places like the Bay of Islands, a deliciously simple string of islets at the top of the country's North Island, are setting the scene with extraordinary hideaways that are one part Robinson Crusoe-style archipelago and nine parts pure luxe. Some of them, such as Awaroa Bay, can only be reached via sailboat, helicopter or – perhaps the best way – a three-day hike through the pristine scenery. Others, such as the

Boatshed on magical Waiheke Island, a collection of perfect, super-luxurious cottages inspired by beach houses and boat sheds of old, offer architecture that celebrates the honesty of form and purity of line (complete with tongue and groove interiors for charm, concertina louvres for cross-ventilation and classical teak steamer chairs for siestas – truly a design that speaks of lazy days on the sand).

And then there are the truly remote places Down Under, such as Wilson Island and Haggerstone Island, which require a series of small planes and a whole lot of stamina to reach. The former is located directly on The Great Barrier Reef, so you can amble down the sand and onto the flotilla of coral for a snorkel before breakfast. Furthermore, it only accommodates 12 in its six designer safari tents, which are really more luxury bungalows than canvas flaps, so there's every chance you can spend the day swinging in your hammock on your own private deck without seeing another soul. The latter, Haggerstone, is slightly more elaborate but still reassuringly understated, and blissfully remote; in fact, it has become a favoured hideaway for one of Australia's former prime ministers.

Woodwark Bay, meanwhile, on the edge of the Whitsunday Islands, is a village-like cluster of coolly serene, super-luxurious huts designed for either a couple or an entire entourage of family guests, should you want to bring them along.

It's sexy and discreet and extravagantly grand all at the same time, and features a collection of dignified dwellings, from a high-gabled 'Main House' to an island hut with an outdoor bathtub, that redefine decadence. Hide away here, and you can almost imagine you have the entire Whitsundays all to yourself.

There are also the wilderness retreats, which are springing up in pristine pockets of each country's rural areas. Tasmania, an island off the coast of Australia that's becoming known for its spectacular scenery, has seen several of them open in the last few years, catering to a new generation of travellers who want invigorating activities and eye-opening hikes as much as log fire-side cognacs and plush luxe.

But perhaps the most innovative escapes are those being created in Australia's Outback region, one of the world's last frontiers. Here, among the vast deserts, wide skies and grand beauty, hoteliers are fashioning extraordinary hideaways that are so eco-sensitive to their surroundings, they almost disappear into the landscape. Longitude 131° at Uluru (formerly known as Ayres Rock) is one of them, and indeed was one of the first to see the beauty in creating a place inspired by its setting. Designed in such a way that it leaves minimum footprints on the land – just as the Australian Aborigines intended – this elegant 'resort' is in fact a string of elevated deluxe tents pivoted toward the famous monolith

to catch the plays of light over the landscape. The intention was to immerse guests completely and utterly in the experience offered by this untouched wilderness without destroying the landscape in the process. A popular activity run by Voyagers Hotels and Resorts is the 'Sounds of Silence' dinner, which takes place at sunset in the desert under the stars while waiters serve a dinner of Champagne and barramundi, and an astronomer takes you on a tour of the Milky Way…

It is these kinds of escapes that are setting a precedent. But they are also catering to a new breed of travellers who want something more than overstyled resorts and hyped-up hotels. With the focus now firmly on individuality, authenticity, originality and integrity, both hoteliers and travellers are searching out destinations that are quieter, more exceptional, and far more memorable.

Remote Luxury is a paean to perfect places to stay. A guide to the most beautiful, most remote, and most luxurious places to get away, it is for all those who desire more out of their destinations, whether it be space, simplicity, understated luxe, grand landscapes, a moment of illumination, or simply a sublime experience.

So pack your bag, and find a spot to call your own….

Janelle McCulloch

OUTBACK

Bamurru Plains

The latest thing in international travel circles is to get right away from it all. Not just a little way away, say, to some beach retreat on the fringes of the city, but right away. So far away, you wonder where on earth you're going.

Bamurru Plains, a three-hour drive from Darwin in Australia's far north, is a perfect example of the new far-flung 'luxury bush' resort popping up like anthills in remote corners of Australasia. Located at the Top End of Australia, this surprising hideaway is a safari-style camp for those who love isolation, intrigue, adventures and enough dramatic landscapes and experiences to keep conversations peppered with colourful adjectives for months. Its location, 5 kilometres from the Northern Territory coast with the famous Kakadu National Park on one side, is a large part of the romance, and indeed was an integral part of the owner, Charles Carlow's plan.

Carlow envisaged a place that was wild and frontier-like, but still had all the comforts and class of a luxury getaway. He designed Bamarru so that guests accustomed to fancy accoutrements would still feel at home – there is a raised, infinity-edged pool, a covered deck with daybeds and elegantly rustic cabins – but left in the necessities of Outback living, including crocodile-proofing the pool, so that people would know

they were still very much out in the wilds. And it's a clever tactic, because jaded travellers seeking new horizons far from deadlines and stress are flocking to these remote stations like brolgas at breeding season.

Along with the remoteness and the sheer audacity and intrigue of this terribly harsh area, part of the key to the success of Bamarru is that, like El Questro, it is a working station, a working water buffalo station, to be precise, and the four-legged inhabitants are as intrigued by the two-legged versions as the latter are about them. Guests normally start the day with a 6am tour of the plains, the savannah woodlands and the paperbark swamps, taking in the animal life, which includes buffalos, crocodiles, wallabies, water pythons, goannas, dingoes and waterbirds by the thousands set against a theatrical backdrop of wide skies, big storms, unusual flora and fauna and blazing sunsets. Lunches and dinners are spent back at camp and can include crocodile or camel canapés, bush tucker, or a barramundi, if a guest has been particularly lucky at fishing the Mary River, which cuts through Bamurru before reaching the sea.

The architecture of the camp itself is pure safari to match the surrounds, although admittedly more 'luxury' than 'rough', and designed to

11

appeal to those who want simplicity with their down-to-earth adventure. The stylish lodge is breezy and open, with an equally open bar and ample places to loaf with a cool drink at the end of the day. (Sunset cocktails are de rigueur here.)

The suites are constructed of materials sympathetic to the environment, including roughly hewn timber beams and corrugated iron, which, rather than appear 'rustic', further add to the atmosphere. In addition, each has been designed so that they not only blend with the surrounding bush but the surrounding bush often blends with them, and guests are often enthralled by the haunting calls of whistling kites or blue-winged kookaburras at dawn. The morning chorus of tens of thousands of magpie geese, after whom the camp is named, is an experience in itself. Thankfully each safari suite is ensuite and raised on a timber platform, so guests don't have to worry about snakes or crocodiles when they sit outside at night. There is also space for sitting out the heat of day with a good book or watching the local wildlife float, fly or wander past.

It is all beautifully, hypnotically, romantic. Indeed, the concept is so distinct that *UK Condé Nast Traveller* magazine included it in the 2007 Hot List of New Properties around the world. With no telephones, TVs, CD players or the typical features of a hotel room to distract you, the focus turns, as it should in such a place, to the animals and environment. The floodplains of the Mary River region, and the wetlands and savannah woodlands that fringe the coastal regions between Darwin and Kakadu National Park, form one of the most significant ecosystems in Australia. The Mary River alone is home to some 236 species of birds, many of which congregate in extraordinary numbers.

A place of marvelous contrasts and rich adventures, Bamurru Plains is a destination for those who want the thrill of the unknown combined with the reassurance of style and guest comforts. In short, it's a journey unto itself.

LANDSCAPE
Wild frontier

ARCHITECTURE/DESIGN
Luxury rustic

BEST VIEW
Back of a ute with a beer at sunset

Burrawang West Station Retreat

Central New South Wales, Australia

The sky over Burrawang West Station is quintessentially Australian: big, blue and tinged with billowing white clouds – a real poetic, Henry Lawson sky. It perfectly suits the homestead that lies beneath it, which is something Lawson, one of Australia's great writers, would have also loved. He would have cherished the landscape too: 10,000 acres of prime cattle country, noted for its rich pastures and picturesque scenery.

Here on 12,000 acres of Lachlan River country in central New South Wales, nestled beneath the big skies and landscape dotted with clumps of romantic gum trees, there is what could be considered one of Australia's most stylish homesteads, a traditional country retreat that has not only redefined the term 'luxury' but completely turned it on its head.

Redesigned by leading Melbourne architects Denton Corker Marshall, this grand property, which once encompassed more than 520,000 acres and boasted one of the state's largest shearing sheds, is now experiencing a new lease of life after its very modern makeover. The striking redesign not only captures the essence of traditional country life and all its iconic Aussie imagery but also offers a cutting-edge glimpse into the future of rural style. The decision to employ a group of urban architects to work on

the outback station – a brave one by the former Japanese owner – has paid off handsomely, because Burrawang is now nothing short of five-star fabulous.

There are still classic farm buildings in abundance here, but they are now more Zen-like. The 'Jackaroo' and 'Jillaroo' guest cottages are so beautifully streamlined, it's as if Giorgio Armani himself had trekked out to the bush to stamp his Milanese style on this very Australian place. Sleek screened verandahs with chic white deckchairs offer a place to contemplate the twilight skies with a glass of something smooth, while marble bathrooms with clawfoot baths provide a luxurious place to wash the dust off at the end of the day. There are also formal gardens to wander in, and the stately, high-ceilinged homestead to stretch your legs out with other guests.

Of course, not everything at Burrawang West has been modernised. In fact, the station's exterior timbers have been left untreated to weather naturally, so that they will eventually turn an elegant grey shade, while certain classic Australian elements, including the aforementioned verandahs, were retained so guests could stare out at the views while sipping their drinks in peace.

Burrawang has, for various reasons, changed hands several times, but thankfully the various owners have realised the vision, and seen the potential of retaining the station's unique style.

Its current owner, a businessman, bought the property in 2000, re-established it as a commercial beef station, now producing the famous Burrawang beef, and finally opened it to the public so everyone could have the opportunity to experience good, old-fashioned Australian hospitality on an outback cattle station – albeit a luxurious one.

At once utilitarian and beautiful, Burrawang West Station is a lavish, qunitessential Australian hideaway that makes you rethink homestead style, while remembering how wonderful life in the country can be.

CONDOBOLIN

BURRAWANG
WEST STATION
RETREAT
●

MULGUTHRIE

23

LANDSCAPE
Wide open plains

ARCHITECTURE/DESIGN
Classic station style but with an
architectural edge

BEST VIEW
From the pier on the riverbank

El Questro

The area around El Questro, in the remote north of the country, offers one of the most romantic images of the Australian Outback to come along since *The Thorn Birds*. It is so romantic that director Baz Luhrmann chose it as the backdrop for the new film, *Australia*, starring Nicole Kidman and Hugh Jackman. If anything is The Last Frontier in this, a world of rapidly fading last frontiers, it is this place: the untamed territory of the Kimberley region of Western Australia. Luhrmann couldn't get much more isolated if he tried.

Here, in this vast landscape of wild orange sunsets, plummeting gorges and waterfalls, craggy mountain ranges, deep blue skies that drift on forever and red earth as far as the eye can see, there are chiseled stockmen, not-so-friendly crocodiles, and extraordinary geographical formations like the Bungle Bungles, Australia's second most visited natural attraction after Uluru (Ayres Rock). It is where man meets Mother Nature at her most untouched.

In the midst of all this vastness sits El Questro, a green, oasis-like place that appears out of the red dirt in such a way it feels like a long, cool drink after a drive through the desert. So far out, in fact, many guests comment that it feels like

"it's right on the edge of the world". In front of the homestead there is the gentle curve of the river – almost surreal amid the arid, furnace-hot landscape, and behind an enormous sweep of wild country. El Questro itself spans a million acres, making its staggering dimensions almost unfathomable for those who hail from quarter acres in the suburbs.

Originally designed to be the home of the two visionaries behind the revamped station, Will and Celia Burrell, the homestead is constructed out of river rock and red cedar, and is surrounded by a lush garden of English lawn and vivid bougainvillea, jasmine and hibiscus, all of which further add to the startling oasis factor. There are only six bedrooms, so the homestead still feels like a private home, and with laundry, liquor and fine wines on the house, you could almost believe you've come to your very rich uncle's place in the Outback for an indulgent stay. There's even a supposedly friendly crocodile in the river – the homestead's very own pet.

The station is actually a working cattle station with a herd of approximately 5,000 head of Brahman and Shorthorn cattle, and closes to guests from November to March each year. The idea, developed by Will and Celia, was to create

27

a successful station where visitors, which have since included Crown Prince Frederick and Princess Mary of Denmark, and Kylie Minogue – could experience Australian life on the land – albeit in luxury fashion. Ironically, when Will, an old Etonian from England, first saw the place, he suggested it was "probably the worst cattle station in Australia". Nevertheless, he paid the owner a million dollars for the lease – the lease, mind, not the freehold – and around 2000 head of cattle, and set about creating his dream. After they conducted a muster, he discovered the countryside was so rugged he actually had around 7000 head.

Still, there was room for more, surmised Will, so he organised to accommodate more – tourists this time – "up here you can run more tourists to the acre than cattle", he once quipped – and El Questro was born.

Activities here are unlike most you find in other places, however. There's barramundi fishing, ravine hiking, bathing in natural springs, night crocodile spotting, or just pouring an icy beer and watching the stars emerge from the ink-black sky. If you're feeling really courageous and up for an adventure you can join one of the guides and cruise by boat up the croc-filled river to see Aboriginal paintings.

This is real *Crocodile Dundee* country: an intoxicating place with heady contrasts and juxtapositions, seen best when you sink into the cool of the rock-pools or the Zebedee Springs after a day in the dry heat of the Outback landscape. But perhaps the best place to be at El Questro is the antique bathtub in the Chamberlain Suite, which hangs 15 metres above the river, allowing its occupants a direct look straight down to the crocodiles and a bird's-eye view of the wilderness spread before you.

DARWIN

EL QUESTRO
HOMESTEAD

BROOME

LANDSCAPE
Top End remote

ARCHITECTURE/DESIGN
Outback glamour

BEST VIEW
From the antique bathtub in the Chamberlain Suite, with the river below

Longitude 131°

Ever since a few enterprising entrepreneurs decided to create a couple of upmarket escapes on the African plains with nothing more than a couple of sheets of canvas and a few luxury accessories, safari-style escapes have become the hottest thing since the Gobi Desert. In Australia, several have emerged, no doubt because much of the country offers a landscape that's perfectly suited to them; and there are plans for still more.

The granddaddy of such camps in Australasia is Longitude 131°. Located atop an isolated sand dune close to the border of the Uluru-Kata Tjuta National Park, home of the fabled monolith, Uluru (previously known as Ayres Rock), this extraordinary bush retreat is designed to leave minimum footprints on the land – as the Australian Aborigines intended – while offering visitors an intimate connection with it. The intention was to 'immerse' visitors utterly and completely into the experience offered in the wilderness of the national park without destroying the landscape as they did so. Thus, the elevated deluxe tents – set in one of the most perfect positions to catch the play of light over the rock and the landscape – have transparent walls that provide an ever-changing narrative of the colours and sky, as well as private views of the sunrises over the engaging rock and the wide horizon behind. Inside, the palatial canvas-topped suites are decked out with every conceivable luxury, from king-sized beds dressed in white linen to writing desks, phones, CDs and air conditioning, so you can experience the Outback without having to suffer from it, and commune with nature without having to, well, commune too much.

It's a far cry from the camping days of old, where hard ground poked through sagging air mattresses and all manner of wildlife wandered in during the middle of the night. There are also no queues for the amenities block. And no lines for the communal barbecues. The elements are still there to contend with, but in winter, when temperatures may drop below zero at night, guests are given a thick doona, and the evening campfire is built up till it roars. There is also a swimming pool, sundeck, a 24-hour bar, and a three-course dinner menu that changes daily and features modern Australian cuisine enhanced by indigenous flavours.

31

Longitude 131°
Yulara Drive, Ayres Rock, Northern Territory, Australia

Phone +61 2 8296 8010

www.voyages.com.au

Longitude 131° is designed to appease both fussy travellers and the 'keepers' of this land, the Aborigines, who wanted these tents constructed to preserve the area's fragile sand dunes. This plan had the unexpected benefit of charming the guests, most of whom weren't too fussed about the luxuries but were thrilled that the camp showed what was obviously minimal impact on an extraordinary environment. It's an eco-sensitive retreat of the most Australian kind, and one for those who want to unwind without any fuss.

34

ALICE SPRINGS

KINGS
CANYON

LONGITUDE 131°
●
ULURU
(AYRES ROCK)

LANDSCAPE
Mystical Uluru (Ayres Rock) magic

ARCHITECTURE/DESIGN
Tented luxury

BEST VIEW
Looking out to the rock at sunset

Rawnsley Park Station

The Flinders Ranges are famous in Australia, particularly among the bush set who like to pack their tents and escape to nature. Majestic, mysterious and reassuringly remote, the region is a spectacular spectacle of sharp ridges and riotous colours. Imagine dirt so red it's the shade of rust, and then transplant it against a sky so blue you almost can't fathom how it can be linked to the same one back in the city. Then add in the impossibly beautiful Wilpena Pound, a natural ampitheatre that is the defining landmark of this area, and you have what is one of the most fabulous Outback escapes in the country.

Set right in the middle of all this fabulousness is the oasis that is Rawnsley Park. This 3000-hectare working sheep station set on the southern face of Wilpena Pound has been popular with Flinders Ranges lovers for some years – the award-winning retreat had already installed a pool, restaurant and camp ground – but recently it has also built four super-stylish eco-villas and the new additions have cemented the 'fab factor' of this fantastic destination.

The Villas incorporate all the latest energy-saving features, including rendered straw bale walls, polished timber floors over suspended concrete slabs and overhanging eaves and wide verandahs to provide shaded walls. They also feature raked ceilings and natural exhaust venting at the apex of the ceiling space to provide natural cooling efficiency, along with carefully placed windows and doors to allow for cross-ventilation.

In addition, each villa is positioned away from the main resort, and pivoted to optimise views, and thus become the main attraction. If that wasn't enough to keep visitors open-mouthed with surprise, the bedrooms feature retractable ceilings, so that you can lie back and stare at the stars all night long. Who knew you could get this close to nature without having to suffer the elements in a tent?

It's a retreat that seems to perfectly suit its richly toned surroundings. The silver roofs that reflect the glare of the sun shimmer in the heat of the day, while the verandahs provide both shade and an elegant place to watch the fading light at the end of the afternoon. Still, most guests are too busy exploring the surrounding region to spend much time indoors. The station's owners, Tony and Julieanne Smith, positively encourage Outback adventures, and offer bikes, horses or hiking trails to stretch your legs on. There are also scenic flights over the mountains, or four-wheel-drive trips through the bush. If you come here and think there's nothing to do or look at, you're just not trying hard enough.

37

Rawnsley Park Station
Wilpena Road, via Hawker, South Australia, Australia

Phone +61 8 8648 0030

www.rawnsleypark.com.au

RAWNSLEY
PARK STATION
●

FLINDERS RANGES
NATIONAL PARK

PORT
AUGUSTA

GLADSTONE

41

LANDSCAPE
Rugged mountain drama

BEST VIEW
On a walk through the Flinders Ranges

PACK
Hiking boots and water

Wrotham Park Lodge

If you want to visit Wrotham Park Lodge between June and August, then get ready to saddle up, because this is when the Outback station's annual cattle muster occurs. You don't really have to join in if you're not accustomed to riding, but it's almost certain you'll still want to be part of the action in some way. There is just something about all that stirring of dust and kicking of hooves that makes the excitement contagious.

Located on a 600,000-hectare property in Queensland's northwest, 300 kilometres west of Cairns, Wrotham Park Lodge is the answer to every adventurer's dream. The working station combines the rich heritage of Australia's rural history with classic cattle station life and a unique resort experience, immersing guests in a variety of activities that range from mustering (by horseback, motorbikes or helicopter) to four-wheel-driving.

The homestead is styled on pioneer designs, but features a distinctly modern edge. The timber slab buildings that make up the bustling centre of the property have wrap-around verandahs, in recognition of Outback architecture, but also feature unexpected luxuries, such as a library and bar. In addition, there is an innovative outdoor living area with a large raised platform designed for pre-dinner drinks and wildlife watching, which is set around the modern version of a camp-fire. This latter feature, when lit, reflects the brilliant reds of the sunsets glowing on the velvet-lined horizon.

There are only 10 guest quarters, but this just makes it feel more like a private station, albeit a very luxurious one. Their style was inspired by stockmen's quarters, although they certainly boast more modern comforts than stockmen used to receive. In fact, the quarters are now more along the lines of what the landed gentry used to live in, with leather armchairs, and shaded verandahs with day beds and squatters' chairs.

Each of these quarters is set along the escarpment and feature expansive decks to take in the sublime views of the Mitchell River. Not that guests tend to spend much time staring, when there is so much else to do. There's fishing, more fishing, gourmet picnics by the river, cattle mustering and yard work, further fishing,

43

WROTHAM
PARK LODGE

CAIRNS

CARDWELL

INGHAM

or just sitting and stargazing with a drink in hand. Just like the pioneers did, only now, you don't need to bed down with a swag.

Wrotham Park Lodge pays tribute to the Outback without framing it and packaging it up in a commercial enterprise. Its hospitality is subtle but gracious, and its atmosphere is elegant but still offers opportunities for wicked adventures. In short, it is the modern-day getaway: rugged, wild, untamed, and committed to aesthetic beauty and environmental conservation as much as architectural innovation.

LANDSCAPE
Queensland Outback at its most dramatic

ARCHITECTURE/DESIGN
Modern pioneer

BEST TIME TO VISIT
June to August, when cattle mustering takes place

ISLAND

Bedarra Island

For many years Bedarra Island's resort was a byword for style, a place where the rich, the very rich, the too famous to name and anyone else who didn't want to be found flitted between the secluded beaches like cicadas on a summer night. Much of this had to do with both the free bar (the Bollinger Champagne, premium wines, top-shelf vodka and other heady cocktail ingredients are gratis) and the architecture. Day beds big enough for a party and decks extensive enough to Tango on set the scene for Bedarra's new style of barefoot luxury, one of the most innovative on the Australian resort scene.

Word of the exclusive island hideaway spread, and the place was quickly embraced by frazzled A-listers, including Jennifer Aniston, Cameron Diaz, Salma Hayek, Catherine Zeta-Jones and Mariah Carey, seeking a respite from fame on a place that appreciated life's more exclusive pleasures. Then, like most parties, Bedarra suffered something of a hangover, as the resort aged slightly. The resort's owners, Voyages, ordered a makeover as slick as any Hollywood star and after a nip and tuck and some more plastic surgery to add swish new villas, the place emerged spectacular again. Even after Bedarra

took a direct hit from Cyclone Larry in mid-2006, Voyages took the opportunity to 'refresh' the place, bringing it up to old Bedarra levels once more.

While some bemoan the island's isolation, and the logistics required to get there (a flight from Cairns, followed by another short flight or ferry to Dunk Island and boat transfer to Bedarra), others relish the seclusion. The 32-guest limit also means there are private beaches, coves and corners for all. Some do elect to order a takeaway hamper and escape to their own secluded alcove for swimming and picnicking but many prefer to stay near their suites. And this is where the resort really excels.

The architecture of the 16 open-air, split-level, two-storey and deluxe pavilions is designed for privacy, with each suite built to blend into the natural rainforest and beach setting. Each also features views of the sea and offers a private terrace, a fully stocked fridge with daily cheese selection, French Champagne, fresh-baked cookies, and snacks and bathrooms with deep soaking tubs and rainforest views. The most coveted places to stay are the The Point and the

49

two glass 'Pavilions', which combine indoor/ outdoor living spaces – one for sleeping and bathing and the other for reading, drinking, snoozing and generally counting the clouds over Wedgerock Bay. Connected by a central sundeck with infinity-edge plunge pools, these glass-walled zones include Bose sound systems, laptops, private bars, floating beds and chic banquettes for reclining in style. Everything you need, really.

While some people dislike the island-style service (no room service, reception closes in the late afternoon and DIY at the bar), others love the

whole Robinson Crusoe-style escape feel about it. And indeed there are parts of the place that are coolly beautiful, not least the shimmering blue plunge pools that are the same perfect turquoise shade as the sea. The day beds are also dressed in an elegant shade of black, matching the designer sunglasses and swimsuits of the celebrities reclining on them. All in all, Bedarra Island is made for louching in luxury. As one guest said: "All you do is sit around all day and sleep, drink and eat." And that suits most people just fine.

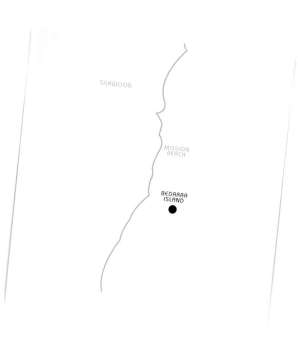

SILKWOOD

MISSION
BEACH

BEDARRA
ISLAND

ARCHITECTURE/DESIGN
Cool class

STYLE
Celebrity escapism

PACK
Very big dark sunglasses

Capella Lodge

When hoteliers James and Hayley Baillie decided to take a slightly dated but still promising resort on a remote island in 2003 and update it for a new generation of do not disturb junkies, the result – Capella Lodge on Lord Howe Island – set a new benchmark for boutique hotels.

More of a contemporary, luxury beach house than a ritzy, glitzy resort, the lodge was modelled on an intimate hideaway for a well-heeled family – sort of a fusion between a luxury New Zealand lodge and a sleek beach villa. In fact, the Baillies still often stand back and wonder if they should convert it into a private retreat for their friends and family ("We often thought of having it just for ourselves," jokes James Baillie), but then the legions of guests who have hidden away here and since befriended the staff and family would no doubt continue to turn up and cajole them into providing a suite.

"Privacy is certainly the main attraction here," explains Baillie, who was the former CEO of P&O Resorts Australia, and the visionary behind the glam-up of similar celebrity hideaways, Bedarra Island and Lizard Island. "Obviously that's what people are looking for now in a seaside hideaway, that as much as style and scenery."

The key is its quiet design. Conceived and built in an architectural style that can only be understated Australian, the lodge was kept deliberately small, so a sense of intimacy and privacy was encouraged, and discreetly hidden in among the kentia palms of Lord Howe's famous landscape so that its footprint was minimised. There is an old Aboriginal adage that says dwelling should touch the earth lightly, and this place barely makes a dent on its spectacular surrounds.

The emphasis here is on the view rather than the resort, and wherever possible expansive decks and walls of glass embrace the vista, which is quite possibly Lord Howe's best. That's not to say the design is uninspired; on the contrary, the Baillies deliberately chose teak timber that would age gracefully to a driftwood grey, without losing its special patina, while the old floorboards – salvaged from a warehouse – will only become more beautiful with the footprints of future guests. And the dramatic skillion roof politely nods to Australia's original beach house architecture but also adds a touch of visual excitement and modern form. "It's important to be unobtrusive," says Baillie. "Good hoteliers are realising this, that it's important to create places

57

that respect their surroundings, and 'weather' the elements as well as them".

Inside, the interior design was intended to be similarly calm and restrained. The coolly beautiful suites, which were also conceived to resemble elegant beach houses, are the picture of chic, and yet have been cleverly designed so that it doesn't matter if you traipse in and scatter grains of sand everywhere. In line with the barefoot chic style of architecture, there are polished timber floors, bleached shuttered doors, charming white tongue and groove walls, bedrooms on mezzanine levels that give them a loft feel, and expansive decks with sumptuous seating areas. Furthermore, each of the suites is thoughtfully fitted out with complimentary backpacks for day trips to the beach, the latest magazines for style junkies, groovy little bottles of pre-mixed Campari and soda, Manfredi coffee, and cushioned daybeds both indoors and out to stretch out on with a good book.

The public areas, including an all-in-one, open-plan restaurant/bar/informal lounge, and a cosy library with fireplace, are just as beautiful, with fabrics from Denmark, prints from Mambo designer Bruce Gould, ottomans made from fired ceramic, wicker lightshades created by craftsmen skilled in fishing baskets and a colour palette of pale pebble, lagoon blue, mountain grey and Kentia palm green that's drawn from the natural hues outside. Judging by the number of guests who prefer to chill out in these areas rather than their private suites, the studied attention to aesthetic detail has worked.

Cool, contemporary, and blissfully civilised, Capella Lodge effortlessly and stylishly combines the best of luxury modern resorts with the easy-going nature of family beach houses, blending simplicity with pure sophistication in a perfectly natural package.

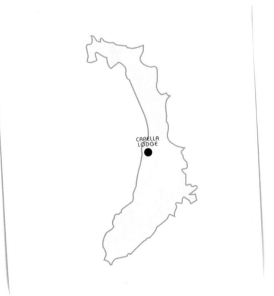

CAPELLA LODGE

LANDSCAPE
Reef-rimmed, Tahiti-style atoll

ARCHITECTURE/DESIGN
Simple beach house meets slick
international design

BEST VIEW
From the deck looking out to Mt Gower
and Mt Lidgbird

Eagle's Nest

Bay of Islands, New Zealand

The Bay of Islands is a world-renowned destination and it's not surprising. Even the name evokes an idyllic cluster of magical islets surrounded by calm blue and bobbing craft. The region is famous for its enchanting coves, secluded beaches and picture-perfect islands, and has become one of the best places to get away, either by boat or by plane. It's also establishing a reputation for deep sea and big game fishing, as well as dolphin and whale watching. In short, it's the dream playground for those who like to be beside the sea.

Amid all this turquoise action, a prepossessing town called Russell has become something of a hub for seafarers and landlubbers alike. The first capital of New Zealand, it is rich in history and old charm, dating back to the days when it was a bustling whaling centre. There is a still a 'marine' feel about the place, assisted by haunts such as the Bay of Islands Swordfish Club, the Duke of Marlborough Hotel, and a collection of famously flavourful fish and chips, and just-as-busy fishing tackle and dive stores. It is a hive of activity, winter, summer, autumn or spring.

Set in among all this seaside splendour is a place that stands out for its luxury touch. The Eagle's Nest is an elegant clutch of luxury beach houses that are more 'modern' than 'old-time', but are no less appealing for it. Designed for groups, who either rent the collection out or just one for themselves and family, it is part of the new style of getaway that's geared towards the 'private villa' feel. Luxury and privacy have become big business in the travel world, with the elite wanting their own 'space' to retreat to without fear of others interfering in their down time, and Eagle's Nest fits the bill perfectly.

The group consists of several distinctly different dwellings, all with just as distinct names. 'Sacred Space' is the central house – a spacious two-storey glass-roofed home with a living area that transforms from relaxed living to formal dining and then into a private movie theatre at night. The 'Eyrie', on the other hand, is situated high up in native bush overlooking the ocean and out to Waitangi, Paihia and the islands of the North. Like 'Sacred Space', it has expansive outdoor living areas to watch the sun set, plus open-plan living areas with all the accoutrements modern

63

Eagle's Nest
60 Tapeka Road, Russell
Bay of Islands, New Zealand

Phone + 64 09 403 8333

www.eaglesnest.co.nz

travellers have come to expect from luxury hideaways, including a plasma screen television and DVD and CD player with surround-sound. There is also an 18-metre horizon-edge lap pool and outdoor spa pool overlooking the bay, to complete the 'mini resort' feel.

And then there's 'First Light Temple', which takes as its cue 'simplicity', but is no less chic in its design. With a mezzanine bedroom, indoor and outdoor fireplaces, an outdoor shower, walls of glass, and bi-fold doors that open onto a balcony on three sides, it is for those who want fine design and easy comfort in equal measure.

67

LANDSCAPE
Sheer drama

BEST VIEW
From the wet-edge pool

BEST TIME TO VISIT
Summer

Haggerstone Island

The stipulation for guests visiting Haggerstone Island, at the very tip of Australia's northeastern coastline, is that they should ideally have some degree of fitness before they arrive. This doesn't mean that they need to be capable of finishing the Tour de France before boarding the plane, but they do need to be able to cope with a degree of physical exertion in order to enjoy the experience.

You see, if the journey to the island wasn't enough (a flight to Cairns, followed by another flight, and then a further boat trip), there's the act of being on the island itself, which involves a certain amount of DIY. This is a place where dishes are not brought to you in a flurry of first-class service but where you have to go out and catch them. Sort of like *Survivor*; only here, you have to pay for the experience.

But Haggerstone's guests don't shy away from these small hitches. Its visitors' book is a roll call of the rich and famous. Former Australian prime minister Bob Hawke loves it so much, he reportedly once visited three times in as many months. There's obviously nothing quite like the back-to-basic charms of Australia's most unusual resort.

Situated in what is possibly one of the most remote locations in Australia, equal only to El Questro and other Outback stations, Haggerstone is a tiny archipelago two hours north of Cairns; and the sheer isolation and beauty of it is quite often a sight for sore spirits. In fact, it is so remote, that it was listed by *Condé Nast Traveller* as the number one destination for the 21st century.

Admittedly, the initial sight of it, with its open Swiss Family Robinson-style house and open rooms dressed in nothing but a handcrafted wooden bed and a mosquito net, does come as an initial shock to those used to a more luxurious style. But very soon a kind of *Gilligan's Island* spirit of adventure sets in, and by the second day most guests are happily paddling about barefoot and offering to help with chores. It's designed to do away with the superfluous details of modern life, and make you realise that you don't need a harbourside mansion and a luxury car to be happy. Indeed, the suggested wardrobe for the island reads like this: cotton shirts, swimsuit, hat, reef shoes and a sarong. It may not seem like much but when you realise that all you'll be doing is snorkelling, swimming and catching something for dinner, it almost seems too much. And because there is no human habitation for some nautical miles, you don't need to worry about the paparazzi hiding behind a tree.

A true island escape, Haggerstone is one part *Survivor*, one part surprise. Yes, it is simple, but sometimes unexpected simplicity can be the ultimate in unadulterated luxury.

69

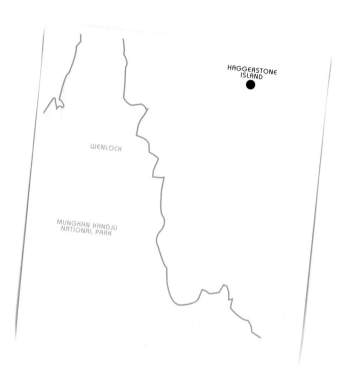

HAGGERSTONE
ISLAND

WENLOCK

MUNGKAN KANDJU
NATIONAL PARK

LANDSCAPE
Robinson Crusoe-style island

ARCHITECTURE/DESIGN
Island-simple, but endearing with it.

BEST VIEW
From the beach with a beach picnic at twilight

Hayman Island

For regular globe-trotters and those who automatically board a plane and turn left, Hayman Island needs little introduction. Australia's luxury resort has been a stand-out on the scene ever since it opened, and for years was one of the destinations of choice for languid jetsetters and the high-at-heel. The pool alone, a lagoon-sized saltwater design that looks from the sky like one of Elizabeth Taylor's emerald rings, has seen more alluring, dark-sunglass-wearing celebrities than just about any other resort in Australia. But, like anything hot, Hayman cooled off for a little while, as the travel rat pack moved on and discovered new horizons. Now, however, after a much-publicised $50 million refurnishment, the place is humming again, and the designer swimsuits and dark glasses are once more out in force.

Set offshore in the northern part of the Whitsunday Islands group, it is not difficult to miss this place as you approach by boat. Everything on Hayman is noticeable, from the enormous, iconic pool to the resort that rises up full gloss mode. The main part of the resort is designed as a string of white-on-white terraces that step down into the palm-fringed lagoon pool. Parts of it do show its age (albeit glamorously), and minimalists might find the slightly over-the-top décor jarring. But on the flipside, the resort has done an outstanding job blending inside and out.

It is in the new part of the resort, however, where Hayman has once again showed that it is a heavyweight force on the luxury retreat scene. The refurnishment included an overall upgrade of the place to reveal more of a clean uncluttered design but the most eye-opening has been the addition of a private Beach Villa fronting Hayman Beach, providing boutique accommodation for those accustomed to a little more privacy for their movie-star dollar. The 90 square metres of absolute luxury – address: Number 1 Hayman, Great Barrier Reef – was designed with local timbers, woven rattan and natural furnishings, and includes private concierge service, an enclosed courtyard inspired by Balinese walled gardens, an outdoor deck with plunge infinity pool, a private outdoor rockery shower, its own refreshment bar, and a state of the art sound system, plus a glamorous bathroom with centrepiece bath and even personalised bathroom amenities.

Hayman Island may be fighting to compete with a new generation of ultra-slick resorts, whose intimacy and smaller size gives them a personalized, private edge over the bigger, glossier destinations, but this grand dame is still showing there is some glamour and glitz left to soak up on this extraordinary island.

73

HAYMAN
ISLAND

HOOK
ISLAND

HIDEAWAY
BAY

WHITSUNDAY
ISLAND

AIRLIE BEACH

PROSERPINE

79

LANDSCAPE
Island-flecked idyll

ARCHITECTURE/DESIGN
High-glam

BEST VIEW
Poolside

Lizard Island

In recent years many upmarket island resorts have introduced daybeds as part of their design scheme, no doubt because, as a design statement, they speak immediately of languorous leisure activities and indolent pleasures; days spent doing nothing but debating the appropriate time to knock the top off the Krug. Indeed, at resorts in Asia, where they first started to make a name for themselves, the sight of them slung along a timber deck in front of a turquoise sea is often enough to send overwrought urbanites into an immediately happy stupor.

For those not familiar with these stylish floating platforms, daybeds are the sexier and cooler version of the sofa: usually big enough to host a cocktail party on and more often than not accessorised with a rattan shade cloth, making them the perfect furniture to pair with a sea view. They are so distinctive in their decadent design that some resorts, such as Lizard Island in Queensland, have literally peppered the architectural landscape with them. In fact, when some people think of Lizard Island now, they immediately think of the daybeds.

But while daybeds are helping to make the name of luxury hideaways like Lizard, it is actually the location of such places that really seals the reputation. And Lizard Island is no exception.

Set 30 kilometres off the coast of Far North Queensland, a comfortable flight from civilisation but far enough away to be free of day trippers, Lizard Island has commandeered one of the best positions a resort could ask for – right on top of the famous Great Barrier Reef. The setting is not only part of the aesthetic appeal, but it allows guests free rein of more than two dozen powdery white beaches, the fringing reef and a piercingly blue lagoon that could have been plucked from a movie. It also offers some of the best scuba diving in the Great Barrier Reef.

Now before you think you're in for an adventurous time on Lizard Island, one thing should be made clear. This place isn't really designed for those who like heart-pumping adrenalin charges. There are no wild nights or heart-stoppingly active days here. (The daybeds attest to that.) Everything about the resort is spectacularly laid back – from the activities to the architecture – and most guests relish every minute of it.

The best place to hole up on Lizard Island and assert your horizontal rights is the Pavilion, a place that, after Lizard's $13-million rebuild in 2003, is virtually heaven redefined. Featuring private decks leading down to its own plunge pool and of course complete privacy and endless

81

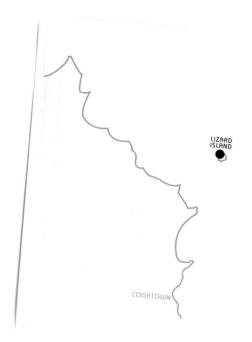

LIZARD
ISLAND

COOKTOWN

views, it also comes with all the modern accoutrements you'd expect, including a laptop, binoculars, and ample Bollinger. If this is too exclusive for the budget, there are the Sunset Point Villas, which offer easy access to a string of secluded beaches, plus a private deck with Australian timber squatter chairs and a hammock – again to get off those aching feet. And if these sound too 'A-list', Lizard also has 40 freestanding villas perched on cliff tops or scattered along under swaying palm trees that are just as elegant, having been built of timber and stone to reflect the natural surroundings. Seamlessly blending indoors and out in a spacious open plan design, many offer a large verandah with – you guessed it – a daybed, just in case you need further prompting.

While some people think Lizard's smartest move was to position itself on this island, a spectacular 1000-hectare national park set right on the reef, there are others who slyly observe that the best thing Lizard's designers did was to lower the centre of gravity. Every few feet you pass a daybed or chaise that quietly commands: "*lie down now*". Talk about the new louche luxe class.

ARCHITECTURE/DESIGN
Island glam

BEST VIEW
From your own daybed

PACK
A glamorous wardrobe

Peppers Palm Bay

The one thing you notice most about the Whitsundays is the water. It's everywhere, carving a cyan swathe through the islands, nudging yacht bows and pier posts and lapping playfully at bathers' toes. Indeed, the watery playground of the Whitsundays is so surreal, so coolly beautiful that it's almost too difficult to digest, much less describe. And it's only when you leave, flying low over that shimmering expanse of ocean sprinkled with its green garnish of islands, that some form of enlightenment occurs, like the aaahhh at the end of a long, cold drink.

For this reason, places like Long Island have always been popular spots for southerners to fly in to for a spot of hydrotherapy and a dash of vitamin D. They offered a place to get some perspective on life; to stare out at all that sea and think of new adjectives for 'happy'. But now there is a new attraction joining the H_2O one and it's the perfect accompaniment to a glass filled with ice. It's gourmet fare of the most delicious kind.

Peppers Palm Bay Long Island is one of the destinations fast establishing a reputation for culinary finesse. Like Noosa to the south, another coastal hotspot that's become popular with foodies and style-philes alike, Peppers is – as its

name suggests – a slice of spice in a place not traditionally known for exotic fare. Its menu veers away from the homogeneity that once defined Queensland cuisine and steers a firm course towards the pluralistic route.

But water and fine dining are not the only things this divine hideaway hidden deep in the Whitsundays has going for it. There are the views, certainly – great sweeping scenes of blue seas, white clouds and idyllic islands as far as the eye can see – but there is also the architecture of this secluded retreat, which makes the most of the cove location and the aforementioned vista. Beautifully designed to embrace the view of blue, the 21 mostly waterfront bures and bungalows may look like Tahitian huts on the outside but inside they're pure sophistication. Rich chocolate and calming beige tones combine to create mini sanctuaries of calm, while the absence of televisions, telephones and alarm clocks means you really do have to relax and let the island entertain you. Part of the package, though, is a hammock with your name on it, so you can swing all day counting the yachts and clouds. Entertainment indeed. If you think you'll get bored with counting clouds, the resort has a mini-movie theatre, swimming pool, tennis

85

courts and spa, but most guests prefer to stay close to the beach and their luxury bures. Even dinner can be served by candlelight on your own private balcony.

With its quiet charm, its isolated island location and its divine architecture and cuisine, Peppers is making a name for itself as a stand-out resort. And in a region that's virtually soaked with them, you can be sure that's saying something.

HIDEAWAY BAY

HOOK ISLAND

WHITSUNDAY ISLAND

AIRLIE BEACH

PROSERPINE

PEPPERS PALM BAY

LANDSCAPE
The ultimate archipelago

ARCHITECTURE/DESIGN
Tucked away luxury

BEST VIEW
From your own hammock out to sea

The Boatshed

What is it about the beach? What is it about being by the coast that makes so many of us drift towards the sea for our annual holidays? Is it the sound of waves crashing at night, which does more for our nerves and insomnia than any chemical remedy? Is it the sight of sand, sea and wet swimsuits, which heartens us more than any city visual? Or is it simply because the sea and all its salty spray enlivens us and makes us somehow feel as if we've stepped away from the everyday, if only for a weekend? Whatever the reason, there are few things closer to our hearts than the notion of the great beach getaway.

The Boatshed, on magical Waiheke Island in New Zealand's north, is a celebration of this collective coastal obsession. Inspired by the yearnings for not only a beach fix but one with an emphasis on simplicity over style – perhaps in a quest to rekindle the spirit of summers past – the owners of this boutique hotel designed a place that was in keeping with the old-world charm of the seaside villages around the country's coastline. The feel is very much of a boat shed, although not a boat shed as most people know it. With chic white tongue-and-groove-lined interiors, big open, airy spaces that seamlessly blend indoors and out, fireplaces to keep the chill off at night, decks that lead down to the beach, its design speaks immediately of lazy days on the

sand. The key to The Boatshed's appeal lies is the elegant simplicity. The cabins are set close to the beach, so close to the water you could dip your toes in before breakfast, while the clever concertina louvres leading to the decks that angle down to the beach open up easily to allow the sea breezes to drift in. In addition, classical teak steamer chairs allow for the mandatory afternoon siestas in the sun. To further add to the beachy spirit, there are complimentary shade umbrellas, sun hats, beach bags, sand mats and sunscreen. So all you need to do is BYO the book and the bubbly.

Reminiscent of a bygone era, The Boatshed is reflective of the quiet life on this incredibly beautiful island. The jewel of the Gulf, Waiheke Island's holiday hamlets and green hills are ringed with beaches, inlets and bays, and the lifestyle is a simple and relaxed seaside one. There are award-winning vineyards and olive groves and lavender plantations, but most visitors are content to simply swim, read, stroll or daydream. And The Boatshed matches the mood perfectly.

A slice of pure charm in a world where resorts and hotels are often too flashy for words, this quietly refined hideaway is unhurried, intimate, exceptionally chic and refreshingly serene.

91

LANDSCAPE
Far-flung island with village feel

ARCHITECTURE/DESIGN
Breezy beach house-style tongue-and-groove
charm, taken up three notches

BEST VIEW
From your own steamer chair

Wilson Island

Wilson Island is what many of us imagine the ultimate island hideaway must look like. It's barely bigger than a hammock, yet still has enough room to escape the few other castaways (maximum: 12) who happen to be sharing the place with you at the time. It's located right on the reef, so you can amble down the white sandy beach and straight on to a flotilla of coral without having to take any overcrowded ferries filled with rowdy day trippers. It's deliciously simple in its architecture, so that no flashy high-rise suites overwhelm the pristine landscape. (There are just six luxury tents, which are sympathetic to the environment while still offering all the indulgences of a splendid hotel.) And best of all, it encourages a generous, friendly frame of mind. The Longhouse, the island's dining room/lounge/meeting place, is made for conviviality, with soft sides that roll down, wraparound banquettes for lounging, and a 15-foot-long communal dining table to encourage conversation at dinner, along with a fridge fully stocked with top-shelf alcohol and an open kitchen where the hosts are known to whip up extravagant feasts. You simply drift in at the end of the day, sand sticking to your toes and sarong still wrinkled from an afternoon siesta

in the hammock, take a seat, and introduce yourself. The resort almost guarantees you will be feeling on top of the world by the end of the night.

The smaller sister of Heron Island, which is also part of the Capricornia group of islands located off the coast of Queensland, Wilson attracts the kind of guests who don't need urban accoutrements to enjoy themselves, which is precisely the kind of person you want to be stuck with on an intimate coral cay. In terms of architecture, it is an 'intelligent' island, which means it is sensitive to its landscape. The tiny cay is so precious, it is super-protected, and so the resort is designed to have virtually zero impact on the environment. The place even closes in February to allow the nesting seabirds some privacy, and indeed at any other time if other wildlife show similar signs of getting intimate with each other.

The tents are more luxury bungalows than canvas flaps but they're still designed to have a low impact on the beach The sheer sight of them, open to the sea but with fresh, white linen for a perfect night's sleep, and with a hammock

97

and timber deck out front, has been known to make some guests sigh with pleasure. There are only 22 paces from each deck to water, so you simply roll out of bed and into the sea to wake yourself up. And if you get sick of the reef, the Longhouse library has dozens of books to keep you amused all afternoon.

If your idea of the perfect resort involves an impossibly beautiful blue sea filled with coral life, the charming simplicity of dining long table-style with a group, and an intimate but still private getaway that's more natural than just about anything else in Australia, Wilson's the ticket.

AIRLIE
BEACH

ROCKHAMPTON

WILSON
ISLAND

NOOSA
HEADS

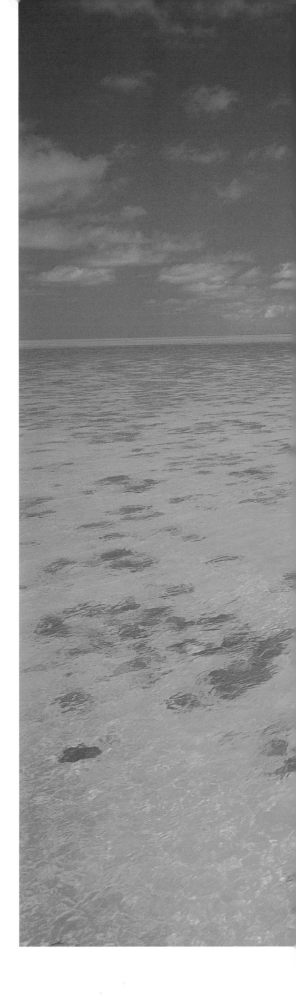

LANDSCAPE
Dream atoll

ARCHITECTURE/DESIGN
Castaway meets high chic

BEST VIEW
Underwater

WILDERNESS

Awaroa Lodge

Awaroa Bay, New Zealand

After years of 'hip hotels' and even hipper hotel guests, there is now a slow but sure shift taking place at the top end of travel. Travellers, seeking new and more distinct experiences than those that just come with a whole lot of global hype are drifting away from over-styled getaways towards quieter, more exceptional places; those with integrity, authenticity and soul that are not only a world away from everything but show an instinctive aversion to the clamour of modern life. *The Guardian* newspaper in London wrote: "[This traveller] is looking for something more ambiguous than culture, history, topological beauty, and relaxation. He is on a mission to [find] the perfect execution of rustic luxe, somewhere with an 'authentic' culture served with a metropolitan slickness." It's a new kind of luxury and it has its base centred firmly on simplicity. As Claus Sendlinger, CEO and president of the Design Hotels group said: "The modern person's notion of luxury is shifting from the opulent and ostentatious to that which is precious and rare – be it time, peace, a moment of illumination, or a sublime experience."

Awaroa Lodge in New Zealand's spectacular south is one of these new kinds of getaway. The ultimate in remote New Zealand hideaways, it is set deep in the heart of the Abel Tasman National Park in Nelson, on the South Island. So deep, it requires a three-day hike to get there. Now, it has become incredibly fashionable of late to have to hike your way to your holiday. The Bay of Fires Lodge first started the trend in Australia, and now several places are continuing it, perhaps because walking to your destination speaks of an escape that's mysterious and distant. Not to mention the fact that it ups your eco-credentials. But Awaroa's remoteness is part of its vision: its mission was to create a place that was not only distinct but preserved the natural setting and promoted sustainable tourism. The walk shows guests just how beautiful the landscape is, while giving them the prolonged anticipation of the experience at the end. Of course you can fly or get a water taxi in, but where's the fun in that? It's known as 'feel-good' travel and it's certainly starting to have an effect on significant numbers of travellers, as hundreds slide on their hiking boots and call for a reservation.

Awaroa is all about being eco-friendly and this applaudable gesture extends to every part of the place. There are recycling and power-generated systems in place, an innovative water disposal, and even an organic garden that supplies produce

105

for the kitchen. The 26 rooms and suites are set discreetly into the native forest, and being devoid of televisions you have to come out of your room to enjoy the scenery. And really, after a three-day hike, you'd want to make the most of the stay. The activities menu is designed for urban voyagers seeking new experiences, from sailing to kayaking (the beach is thankfully only a two-minute walk away), and there is a feast of fine, freshly grown organic food to tuck into at the end of all that exercise at the close of the day.

Perfectly wild and yet thoroughly modern, Awaroa Lodge is part of a new travel culture that's not only eco-conscious but experiments with new ways to appreciate it. The architecture might be discreet, but the experience is right on the edge.

LANDSCAPE
Remote national park wilderness

ARCHITECTURE/DESIGN
Eco-friendly

PACK
Lots of energy

Bay of Fires Lodge

Tasmania, Australia

The extraordinarily varied landscapes of Australia have inspired some extraordinarily different escapes, but the Bay of Fires Lodge is in a class of its own. It is so unique that it has since spawned a host of imitators, but it is still, and always will be, one of the best. It's certainly up there in the top ten places to get away, in fact, so far off the beaten track that you have to hike for two days to get here. It is, quite literally, a walk on the wild side.

Conceived by architect and eco-tourism operator Ken Latona, the lodge is located far from anywhere – and anyone – in the pristine wilderness of Tasmania. Pristine is an overused word in travel but this part of the world really is about as close to untouched as you can get. The only other living things you're likely to see are hopping wallabies and a theatrical display of whales and dolphins at play. Rush hour is non-existent here. Unless you count a wombat or two crossing the path.

The downside, if you can call it that, is to reach such pristine pleasures you have to tug on your hiking boots and walk. Admittedly, it's not too rough, with guides and chefs on hand to cook for you enroute. And there is the scenery – beach after beautiful beach, with squeaky clean sand and

views that constantly remind you how amazing untouched landscapes can be. There is also the reward for all this hard work: a lodge that's unlike anything you can imagine. Or, indeed, have probably stayed in.

The recipient of just about every award in the book, this spectacular piece of architecture – a virtually transparent pavilion – hangs like a spear over the beach. It doesn't so much sit on the landscape as gently float above it, thus reducing any strain on the environment. The style of architecture has the added benefit of enhancing the view for those inside, with one end of the building shaped into a cantilevered balcony that's perfect for standing on with a well-deserved drink to enjoy the breezes and sea vista at the end of the day. (The rest is a discreetly hidden building comprising ten double guest rooms, a library, a living room and a glass-sided dining room.)

It's a sympathetic design that's truly sensitive to its site, with roof-water collection and grey-water treatment systems among the sustainable features. Even the electricity is solar-generated, while the restrooms are organic, and the showers require a bit of a pump to get the water going. If that's likely to put you off,

109

you probably don't belong here, since most of the activities – including sea-kayaking and of course hiking – require some sort of muscle.

But if you think it's all bush and bare basics, think again, because the food is as sophisticated as any city restaurant. And the views are pure heaven.

The Bay of Fires Lodge is part of a new style of resort emerging on the global landscape; one in which abstinence is more important than over-indulgence. Euan Ferguson, writing in the *London Observer*, said of his experience after visiting here: "It is so remote, so beautiful, that I don't want anyone else to know its precise location." Somehow, even if people do, I don't think the Bay of Fires will lose its authenticity and appeal any time soon.

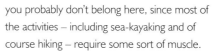

LANDSCAPE
An isolated beach, three days' hike from civilisation

ARCHITECTURE/DESIGN
Intelligently thought out to make minimal footprint

BEST VIEW
On the trek there

Cradle Mountain Lodge

Tasmania, Australia

Cradle Mountain Lodge is designed for the hardier kind of traveller. For a start, there is the alpine climate, which can change moods so suddenly it's often wise to bring a jacket, even if you're only stepping outside to take a quick photo. Then there is the scenery, which verges on the 'dramatic' side, rather than the serene, beachy one. And lastly there are the activities, which range from those requiring walking shoes, warm socks and binoculars, to those that need the full gamut of gumboots and waterproof parkas. On the other hand, Cradle Mountain Lodge does have all manner of luxuries, ranging from roaring log fires to toast your chilly feet after a brisk afternoon hike, a gorgeous lounge that's more like a private member's club (more roaring fires and leather armchairs), and the best thing of all, the Highland Restaurant, which is recognised as one of Tasmania's finest dining experiences.

In short, Cradle Mountain Lodge has combined wilderness and luxury in one, to provide an utterly different experience for those who want to be challenged and inspired. There is so much to do; from trout fishing to mountain biking and alpine hiking, that, after all these outdoor activities, you end up feeling more invigorated than when you came.

The place is famous in Australia for being one of the most beautiful destinations to escape to for some scenery and good, old-fashioned fresh air. Indeed, there is rarely anyone in the lodge during the day because they're all out taking in the views. It's at the end of the day that they drift back to base, tired, hungry and happy, where they change and wander down to the tavern, the lounge or the restaurant for a hearty red and a taste of Tasmania's finest produce. Some retreat to the spa for a sauna, steam room session, hot tub plunge or dip in the cool pool. But mostly guests like to sit by the fire and then retire to bed early, so they can get up early the next morning, tug on their boots and do it all again the next day.

A destination for rejuvenation, Cradle Mountain Lodge is 90 parts pure scenery, 10 parts luxury. And most people prefer the former to the latter.

113

LANDSCAPE
Rocks, mountains, and pure fresh air

ARCHITECTURE/DESIGN
Calm luxe

PACK
Hiking boots

Tarraleah Lodge

Tarraleah was always going to be an ambitious idea. The lodge and village in the heart of Tasmania's Highlands has been around since 1937, and has survived a long, complex and slightly controversial life – some would even say a saucy one. It began its existence as Tarraleah Chalet, a stately showpiece for Tasmania's pioneering hydro electricity operations in the Central Highlands, and, with its dramatic aspect above a wild river gorge, was a suitably magnificent meeting point for officers and management to get together over pipes and port. Eventually, the need for the hydro workers ended and the lodge and its village were left to become a ghost town.

Then, an entrepreneurial type who liked to get her kicks from being a dominatrix came along, took one look at the remote location and the potential for thrills, and took charge, so to speak. She began advertising bondage weekends and reportedly led rounds of nude golf through the historic hallways. The neighbours were not amused, although apparently the woodcutters nearby didn't mind dropping over for a cup of sugar.

In 2005, Tony Harrison and Julian Homer stumbled across the place, took note of its Art Deco beauty and superb location, not to mention the trout-stuffed lakes nearby, and decided to buy it. They injected $10 million into it, refurbishing the lodge and its original 1930's craftsmanship. The eventual transformation saw the place become a super-luxurious retreat, complete with edgy design and the latest in modern communication. The makeover was so successful that the lodge proceeded to pick up dozens of accolades, from a coveted inclusion on *Conde Nast Traveler* US magazine's 'Hot list 07' to a mention in *Condé Nast Traveller* UK as 'One of the Best 65 New Hotels in the World'.

And the media ticks are well-deserved. The sublime new hideaway features luxurious guest rooms with king-sized beds, silk-filled doonas, soft mohair throws, bespoke furniture and indulgent bathrooms complete with spa baths and heated floors. Many of them also have fires and private balconies.

The main part of the lodge is also spectacularly handsome – its highlight is a welcoming library in which guests can sample more than 70 single

117

Tarraleah Lodge
Wild River Road, Tarraleah, Tasmania, Australia

Phone +61 3 6289 1199

www.tarraleahlodge.com

TARRALEAH
LODGE

BOTHWELL

KEMPTON

MT FIELD

HOBART

malt whiskies and super premium cognacs. The Wildside Restaurant offers a choice of over 300 cellared Tasmanian and iconic wines. Reason enough to visit the place.

Sitting high on a ridge overlooking the Tasmanian wilderness, it is a lodge that matches its landscape for pure drama. Up here in the Highlands, the scenery is more spectacular than you can imagine, even after seeing images of it.

The air in Tasmania is said to be among the purest on earth; full of grace and beauty, the almost untouched wilderness is a breath of fresh air for people accustomed to crowds and noise and pollution. There is space to breathe here, among the rivers, lakes, hills and wooded valleys far below. Ten minutes into a visit at Tarraleah, all you can think is: well, it's a good thing the management and the raunchy weekenders moved out, so the rest of us can enjoy it!

LANDSCAPE
Tasmania highlands

ARCHITECTURE/DESIGN
Restored Art Deco

BEST VIEW
While trout fishing

Treetops Lodge

Rotorua, New Zealand

Treetops Lodge is a little like something out of *Lord of the Rings*, only a very modern-day version.

Set deep in the forest of New Zealand's North Island, it is the fantasy of owner John Sax, who envisaged a striking, almost mythical hideaway far from anything but close to nature. He wanted something with a sense of purity, an escape that didn't disturb the landscape with its man-made architecture but sat quietly within it, surrounded by spectacular waterfalls, verdant ferns and pristine bushland. In short, a Middle Earth for jaded travellers. And as a fisherman, ardent outdoorsman and naturalist, he understood the value in keeping New Zealand's natural environment as untouched as possible. He knew that its potential lay in not only the location but also the fact that it somehow preserved the area.

More than three decades on, Sax finally found his land. It was an area of New Zealand's North Island that was home to both virgin native forest with 800-year-old giants, seven crystal-clear spring-fed streams cascading through the forest, and myriad wildlife and flora. He devised a name, 'Treetops', and set about building a fantasy. He

planted 130,000 trees on acreage that had been logged, restored wetlands, and then, together with Californian architect Michael Helm, designed an eco-conscious lodge that sat high in a forest clearing overlooking a valley.

The result is a destination, and a landscape, that has since become steeped in legend. Indeed, it is almost a fantastical escape for those searching for adventure of the highest kind.

In its storybook setting, the architecture is one part *Hansel and Gretel* and one part contemporary country. Its style is derived from this country's pioneering past, and as such the dominant materials are timber and stone, both of which echo the beauty and simplicity of the great outdoors. There are 2500 acres of game reserve to wander around in, including 70 kilometres of hiking or horseback trails. Guests can also indulge in trout fishing, mountain biking, and the latest thing, a Maori Indigenous Food Trail.

For John Sax, Treetops is not only the fruition of a long-held dream, but a chance to show New Zealand's natural beauty to the world, while preserving it for the future.

123

Treetops Lodge
351 Kearoa Road RD1, Horohoro
Rotorua, New Zealand

Phone +64 7 333 2066

www.treetops.co.nz

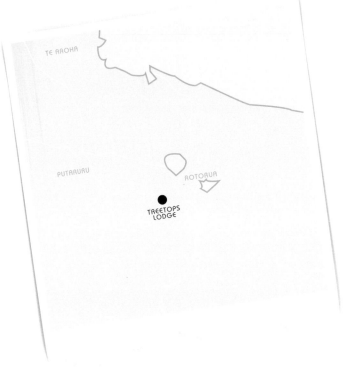

BEACH

Everything about Kauri Cliffs has a revitalising feel about it, even if fortifying weary guests wasn't the architects' sole intention. The scenery is a reviving vision of every green and blue imaginable, from the golf course that rolls down to meet the sea to the splendid forest that surrounds the plantation-style architecture. The activities positively encourage invigorating stretches (even the golf course will test your legs). And the architecture of the lodge is designed so that each suite has its own private verandah, where you can sit and take in the inspiring scene. It's a breath of fresh hotel air in a world where destinations are often more about the 'hip' factor, the stark architecture, or staff who are more beautiful than the guests. Here, it's all about the scenery.

One of the most notable destinations in New Zealand, Kauri Cliffs is as famous for its position as much as its style. It's located right at the very northern edge of the North Island, four hours' drive from Auckland (or an hour by helicopter), where it's perched on a cliff overlooking the Pacific and edged by thousands of acres of hilly farmland. The far-flung resort and its equally famous golf course are the creation of Julian Robertson and his wife, a former Wall Street financier who stumbled across the property while taking time out to write a novel. He was so smitten by the site – even though back then it was only a cattle farm – that he dropped the idea of writing a book and started an idea of doing a luxury getaway. Who knows how successful he would have been at writing, but Kauri Cliffs is certainly testament to his talents as a hotelier.

The key to the success of the place, apart from the famous golf course, is the discreet architecture, which is not only a world away from modern styles but doesn't battle with the landscape for attention. A quiet mix of colonial grandeur and coastal charm, it has a calm, unruffled sophistication about it. Everything here is elegant, and of the 'Assured Taste' school of decorating, which perfectly suits those celebrities who come here to get away from the sometimes over-the-top and tasteless excess of Hollywood. That doesn't mean that Kauri Cliffs has gone completely minimalist in its quest for understated elegance. On the contrary, the obsession with detail means that the lodge even has 'security' rooms for bodyguards and drivers, which, by the way, are just as good as any plush digs a star might stay in. Not that many people are lounging around in their rooms. Most are out on the greens, going for invigorating walks or swims. There are three beautiful beaches out front of

133

134

Kauri Cliffs and acres of inland forests behind, through which the golf course meanders. The entire estate is 6500 acres, so there is enough space if you want to get right away from everyone. And then when you do finally decide to return to base, you can light the open fire in your suite, and then relax by either it (in a beautiful sitting room) or out on the verandah, absorbing the view. With a panorama that includes Cape Brett and the Cavalli Islands, it doesn't get any better.

LANDSCAPE
On the edge

ARCHITECTURE/DESIGN
Unobtrusive but elegant

BEST VIEW
From the greens

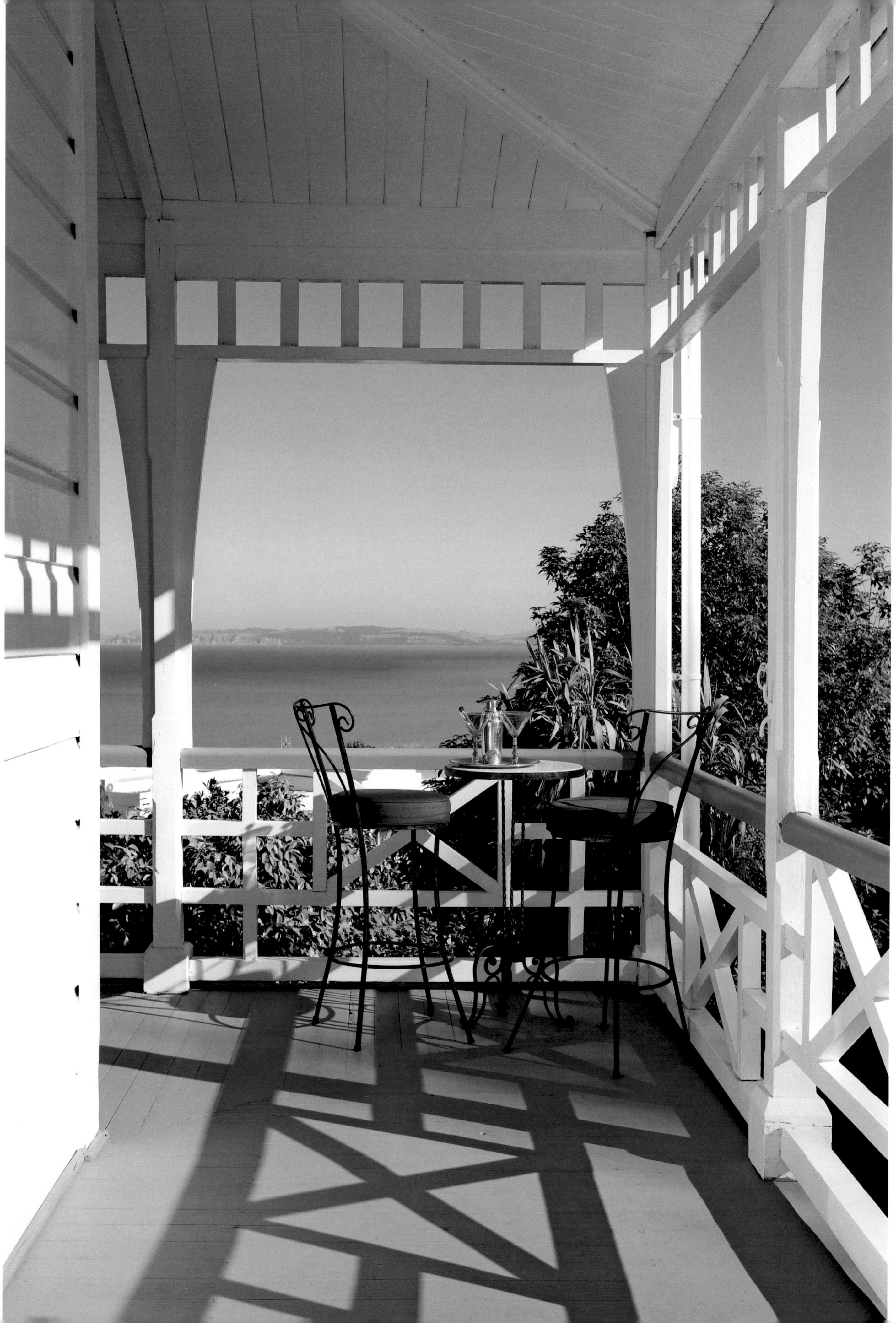

Masters Lodge

Napier, New Zealand

The owners of Masters Lodge, who describe it as 'the smallest luxury hotel', never intended to be hoteliers. Larry and Joan Blume, a former lawyer and dentist from New York, bought the lodge in April 2003 on impulse while they were holidaying in New Zealand. It was difficult to resist, they say. And it's easy to see why.

The historic building, which was once home to Gerhard Husheer, a legendary figure in Hawke's Bay, sits perched on Napier Hill in a direct line of sight with the seafront and Marine Parade. Immensely wealthy by the standards of any provincial city, Husheer was one of New Zealand's richest men by the early 1930s, having made his fortune from the establishment of the tobacco industry in New Zealand. During his life, his house reflected his wealth, with elaborate leadlight windows in Louis Comfort Tiffany designs of fruit and flowers, Art Deco doors, Art Nouveau brass door handles and plates, Arts & Crafts fireplaces, and Charles Rennie Mackintosh leadlights, carvings and appliqués. When she visited many years later, *New York Times* writer Carol van Grondelle described it as a "Fabergé egg set in the industrial tundra of a working port".

In addition to the main house, Husheer purchased Cliff House next door as a servants' quarters before acquiring further land, sloping down the hillside and out to a dramatic point overlooking the Pacific and Cape Kidnappers, in order to construct a gazebo and a retreat house. Another guesthouse was added by acquiring another house to the rear of Cliff House. The combined properties were landscaped and planted with trees, predominantly the New Zealand natives that he so admired, and these in time created a unique park over which his house commanded stunning views of Napier's Marine Parade and the Heretaunga Plains.

When the Blumes bought this grand estate, though, it was in need of some restorative work. So they began lovingly restoring the glamorous interior, decking it out with whimsical and curious accoutrements, such as such as license plates from Husheer's chauffeur-driven fleet of cars, and 1930 drawings for the house renovation by New Zealand Architect Louis Hay, while bringing the exterior and grounds up to their former glory. The result is a destination that has been named one of the Five Best Art Deco Hotels in the World by *The Independent News* UK, as well as one of New Zealand's Top 10 Experiences by *New Zealand Travel Ltd* and one of the Top Ten Gourmet Getaways in the World by *Luxury Travel Magazine*.

139

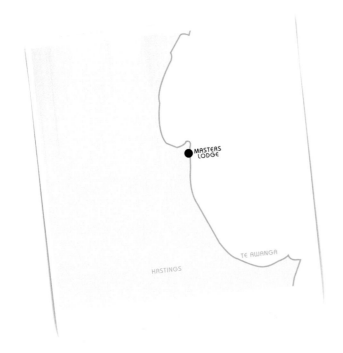

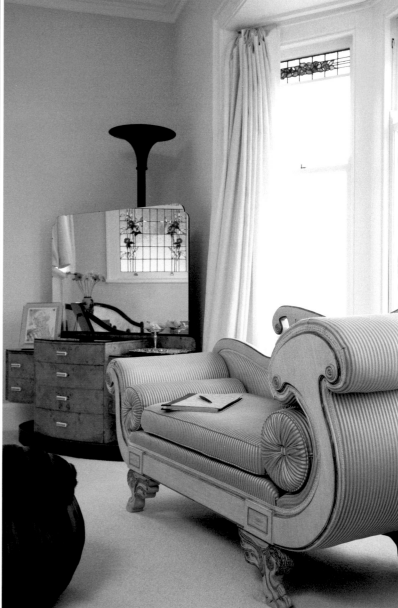

LANDSCAPE
Pure New Zealand drama on the edge of
Hawke's Bay

ARCHITECTURE/DESIGN
Lovingly restored Art Deco

STYLE
Suited to gourmands, view finders and
those who just want to get away

Palazzo Versace

The Versace name needs little introduction to the kinds of travellers who choose destinations based on their glamour quotient as much as their geographical location and reputation. The first foray into the hotel scene for the Versace group, a clever move that has now inspired other designers such as Giorgio Armani and the houses of Bulgari and Ferragamo to follow, the Palazzo was always intended to be lavish, extravagant, and very Versace. The $300-million hotel was the brainchild of Austrian-educated architect Soheil Abedian, whose fascination with the Baroque style and Neoclassicism prevalent in the late Renaissance in Europe during the 17th and 18th centuries led him to envisage a highly ornate escape – and who better to collaborate on such a project than the venerable house of Versace?

As you would expect, almost everything in the Palazzo bears the Italian designer's insignia, from the plates and glassware to the toiletries, towels, linens, rugs, cutlery, and even the artwork. If you need anything further to fill out your Versace stay, there is always the Versace boutique downstairs to assist. Just in case you want to match your underwear to the room.

Unlike other designer hotels, where the brand presence is subtle, if glimpsed at all, here every piece of furniture and fabric, every lion's head and chandelier, is unmistakably Versace. Everything was imported from Italy, from the marble – all $11.5 million of it – to the river stones in the porte-cochère to the massive antique chandelier in the lobby. This 750-kilogram chandelier once hung in the State Library of Milan and was purchased by the late Gianni Versace for one of his villas before being transplanted here, to serve as the centrepiece for the hotel.

The mosaic in the driveway, meanwhile, is the second-largest pebble mosaic in the world after Parliament House in Rome, and was created by five Italian master tilers with an average age of 65 years. Each tiler, from a different region in Italy, handpicked pebbles from their local area to comprise the enormous stone image. Elsewhere, vaulted ceilings are hand-detailed in gold while just about everything else is inspired by Baroque or Renaissance styles. Even the ornate Renaissance-style foyer is flashy with a capital 'F'. It's 'excess all areas', as the paparazzi would say.

145

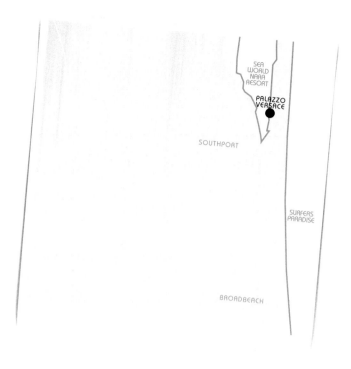

SEA WORLD NARA RESORT
PALAZZO VERSACE
SOUTHPORT
SURFERS PARADISE
BROADBEACH

Opened to Versace-esque fanfare in 2000, the 277-room hotel is situated – where else – on Australia's Gold Coast, an area famed for its beautiful beaches, its corridor of flashy high-rises, and its over-the-top lifestyles. But strangely, the ornate, décor of the hotel seems to suit the surrounds, which are similarly uninhibited. Everything here is of the 'look at me' school, including the guests, who are often as beautiful as the hotel. Ironically, the members of staff are the most subtly dressed people in the place; their understated black tees give them a casually chic rather than overtly stylish look.

Perhaps because it proudly shows off its gilt, glitz and glamour in an age where so many other places are electing for fierce minimalism and pared-down luxury, the courageous flashiness of the Palazzo Versace is endearing. It's one part

Milan, one part Miami, and two parts hedonist's delight. Most of it is utterly extravagant – even the beach is man-made and flanked by the requisite hem of palm trees while the 65-metre swimming pool is modelled on a lagoon – but the gilt grows on you. And the indulgence of choosing from a menu of six pillows is enough to 'soften' anyone into submission.

The Palazzo has certainly appealed to a section of the market – the more private part of the development, the 72 condominiums, have been snapped up by those who love a bit of marble and mirror in their lives. And, of course, the people-watching is perhaps the best on the Gold Coast.

The Palazzo Versace may not be to everyone's taste but there is a lot to be said for its vibrant style. It almost makes beige look boring.

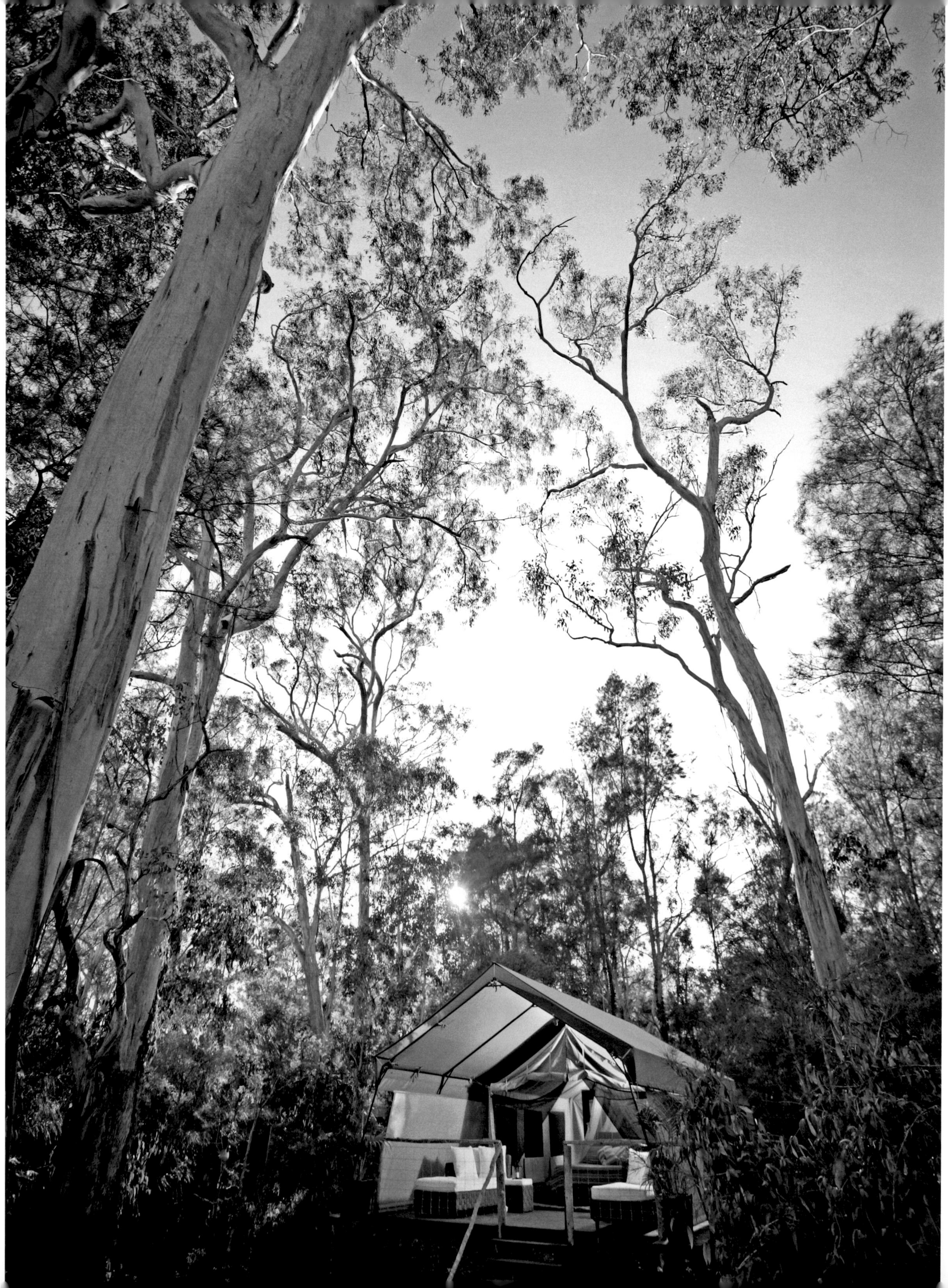

Paperbark Camp

Jervis Bay, New South Wales, Australia

Upmarket, safari-style camps with luxury touches are nothing new. African operators have been doing them successfully for years, with travellers embracing the back-to-basics architecture and the up-close-and-personal experience with the wildlife. Here in Australia, Longitude 131° in the Outback is still perhaps the most famous but it is now joined by some impressive newcomers. Paperbark Camp, at Jervis Bay, on the New South Wales south coast, is one of them.

Taking the principles of safari escapes, this surprising getaway is a clever coastal haven that blends bush and beach in spectacular fashion. Located just a few kilometres upstream from the beach, the camp has been built among a collection of spotted gums and paperbark trees, which have been hand-cleared in order to leave few footprints on the surrounding landscape. The elevated tents that were erected in their place blend just as well into the environment, but feature all the comforts of a luxe lodge. There are wraparound verandahs, double canvas roofs,

luxury cotton linen and pure wool doonas. Energy is solar powered. But before you start thinking that things might be getting too civilised, don't worry, because there are candles, insect screens and handcrafted bush furniture to make you feel as though you are truly going 'back to nature'.

The central meeting place for the camp is slightly more luxurious, with a log fire for winter and an outdoor verandah for summer, but there are still dozens of possums scampering around to remind you that you are in a natural setting.

Paperbark Camp is for those who want to unwind without fuss: if you want to use the 'Do Not Disturb' sign here, you merely unfold the flap of your tent. With bushtucker cuisine, spectacular snorkelling, sea kayaking, bird, whale and dolphin watching, and all the fishing you can handle, it really is a retreat of the most Australian kind: a place where easy simplicity meets pure sophistication.

151

Paperbark Camp
Huskisson, South Coast, New South Wales, Australia

Phone +61 2 4441 6066

www.paperbarkcamp.com.au

152

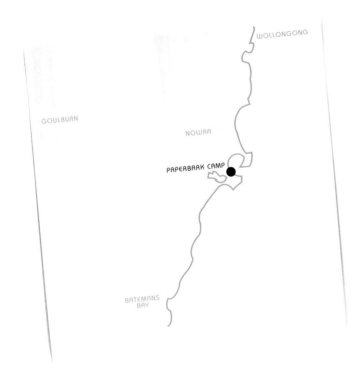

GOULBURN

WOLLONGONG

NOWRA

PAPERBARK CAMP

BATEMANS BAY

LANDSCAPE
Pure Aussie bush

ARCHITECTURE/DESIGN
Luxury canvas

PACK
Mosquito repellant

Woodwark Bay

Islands. They're the epitome of ultimate wealth. Richard Branson has one. Two, if you count the purchase in Noosa River. So does Johnny Depp, Diana Ross and David Copperfield. Vitamin millionaire Vaughan Bullivant and wine mogul Bob Oates have each bought their own Queensland version in recent years, while writer Edward de Bono once boasted four in his property portfolio, claiming they were cheaper and less trouble than wives. It's not surprising that islands are popular since the very word connotes hedonistic decadence and hypnotic pleasures – margaritas until dawn and bikinis at breakfast. Island life brings to mind Noel Coward in Jamaica, Hemingway in the Keys and Ursula Andress rising out of the sea in nothing much at all.

Fortunately for those of us who dream of such idylls but don't have the offshore funds to splash about, archipalego escapes are becoming increasingly affordable. Even the most luxurious, exclusive versions, where you virtually have the entire island all to yourself, are just about within reach for families who choose to share the bill. Furthermore, many places are now being designed to cater for large groups, should you wish to bring your entourage along, whether it's your stylist and co, or simply the rest of the family in tow.

Woodwark Bay in Queensland's Whitsunday Islands, is one such destination. The ultimate island escape, this cluster of luxury huts is like a miniature Aman resort, but just for you. Set on more than 4000 acres of spectacular land, it has accommodation for up to 14 guests, although 'accommodation' is perhaps too pedestrian a word in this instance.

There is the 'Pebble House', which offers two bedrooms separated by a galley kitchen that opens onto the lawns bordering the bay; the 'Island Hut', which allows you to swing in the verandah hammock, or recline side by side with your other half in a bathhouse screened by a palm forest; the 'Siamese Huts' – two huts joined by a wide raised deck looking over the lawns and gardens to the bay; the 'Honeymoon Hut', which is naturally blissfully private; and the 'Main House', a beautiful, thatched, high-gabled communal building that commands stunning views of Woodwark Bay. It is this latter place where guests gather – usually on the deep verandahs looking seaward, in the dining room, or on deep couches inside – to begin or to recall the events of the day.

While the interior of these quietly stylish hideaways are cool and serene, outside the place shimmers with colour and tropical life. Palm trees

159

drip with beauty, beaches beckon with turquoise persuasion and time is something that only comes into effect when you're wondering when it's most appropriate to slide away for a siesta. Woodward Bay is the kind of place you image celebrities and A-listers escaping to for a spot of R&R after, say, an Oscars win or a particularly gruelling film. It is sexy and discreet, and, best of all, makes you feel as though you have the whole of the island, if not the Whitsundays, all to yourself. You may not own the place, but for a few days, you can almost imagine that you do.

WOODWARK BAY

MANDALAY

SHUTE HARBOUR

SOUTH MOLLE ISLAND

LANDSCAPE
A quiet cove the Whitsunday Islands

ARCHITECTURE/DESIGN
Cool, serene, perfect — beach cabins with
a five-star feel

BEST VIEW
From the verandahs overlooking the sea

RAINFOREST

Cockatoo Hill Retreat

Like that old real estate adage, 'location, location, location', Cockatoo Hill Retreat has found what is surely one of the best positions for a hideaway in Far North Queensland. This spectacularly sited getaway is situated in a box seat for viewing nature on the very top of a rainforest ridge in the heart of the Daintree-Cape Tribulation World Heritage area. There are views from Hutchinson Hill towards Cape Tribulation and the Coral Sea to the east, and to the dramatic heights of Thornton Peak in the west. And in between you and all these views, there is nothing but some of the richest rainforest life in the area, from reclusive cassowaries to more colourful and far less shy Ulysses butterflies.

To make you feel even more in the top of the clouds, the 'Tree House' suites comprise private thatched-roof dwellings that redefine the term 'inspiring'. There are more views here, of course, right across the the horizon of the Coral Sea, but there is also plush luxury, from a hand-crafted timber king-sized bed enveloped in a swirl of netting to underfloor lighting, an ensuite and a

balcony for the sea breezes. It's an intimate setting that puts you firmly in the front seat for the ever-changing opera that is the Daintree forest and its myriad feathered inhabitants. Most guests don't need alarm clocks, having already woken to the chorus of birds and the sun rising over the ocean. The main lodge and pool are also designed to put you in touch with nature, with the latter featuring a wet-edge design and cascading waterfall, and the former a thatched roof crafted in the traditional Balinese style, with a bar created from 142 individual cuts of rosewood mahogany. But while the retreat is sleek, the emphasis here is firmly on the wildlife and it's understandable when the area is known for its superb biodiversity. Indeed, new species of rainforest plants are still being discovered in tracts thought to be 135 million years old.

Managed by two nature lovers, Carmen and Gilles, whose intimate knowledge of the Daintree region and its environment adds to the experience, Cockatoo Hill Retreat is both memorable and special.

169

THORNTON
BEACH

●
COCKATOO
HILL RETREAT

171

LANDSCAPE
Ridgetop in the Daintree's rich forest

ARCHITECTURE/DESIGN
Slicked-up tree house

BEST VIEW
From your balcony amid the treetops

Crystal Creek Rainforest Retreat

The area around Crystal Creek Rainforest Retreat is a walker's version of Shangri-La. It is, quite literally, a Garden of Eden; a Nirvana for those who love nature. There are vast tracts of old growth rainforest and World Heritage national park featuring giant strangler figs and 300-year-old rainforest trees, pristine fern-lined gorges, and creeks filled with chilled mountain waters that are so spectacular they look like a backdrop for a mineral water advertisement. Here, if you want to go for a stroll you just pick a park from one of the surrounding national parks. Just fill up your water bottle and get ready to embrace the beauty.

The owners of the enchantingly named Crystal Creek Rainforest Retreat noticed all of this natural splendour and, understandably, fell head-over-fern in love with it. Securing 350 acres, they set about designing a retreat that would take guests away from everything, and drop them in an earthy version of Utopia. Surrounded on three sides by the Numinbar Nature Reserve, which adjoins the Springbrook National Park, the retreat now allows visitors to get up close and personal with the wonders of a World Heritage-listed national park (the owners agreed to protect 75 percent of the property as pristine bushland) and, more importantly, stretch their legs out in the grandness of it.

The northern part of New South Wales has long been associated with renewal, revitalisation, and revival — it was the site for a Woodstock-style festival at Nimbin that encouraged peace, love and serenity (among other things), and Crystal Creek continues the tradition by encouraging guests to shed their city stresses and breathe in the fresh air. There are even hammocks slung over the creek to inspire long periods of forest-gazing contemplation.

The architecture of Crystal Creek is subtle, but not dull. The seven self-contained bungalows include the Glass Terrace Bungalows, which are open-plan cabins almost totally surrounded by glass that allow uninterrupted views of the rainforest; Rainforest Canopy Bungalows, which are intimate split-level designed cabins with oak-lined curved ceilings, expansive windows, and decks; and Creekside Spa Bungalows, which are pitched-roofed bungalows set down in the thick rainforest. None of them have skimped on luxuries, with most including covered decks with barbecues, intimate double spa baths with floor-to-ceiling windows overlooking the rainforest, galley-style kitchens, flat screen TVs and full sound system with iPod docking stations. So for those who are not inclined to wear boots and get sweaty, there is more than enough luxury inside each cabin to keep you amused for days.

173

LANDSCAPE
Old growth rainforest

ARCHITECTURE/DESIGN
Fancy eco-cabins

BEST VIEW
From the hammocks slung across the creek

Daintree Eco Lodge & Spa

Daintree, Queensland, Australia

Set in 30 acres of lush ancient rainforest in the World Heritage Daintree National Park, the highly luxurious Daintree Eco Lodge & Spa has been designed to impeccable standards, with marble floors, timber and bamboo furniture, and sumptuous tiled bathrooms. More importantly than this, however, it has been designed to be friendly to its ultra-sensitive environment. Accommodation is courtesy of 15 treehouse villas that sit neatly and unobtrusively under the canopy of the forest; their bases barely making a dint in the landscape. The minimal development hasn't meant a scarcity of luxuries though, with most of the villas fitted out with chaise longues draped in rich fabrics, four-poster beds, and even marble fittings. A handful of the cabins have outdoor spas and mosquito-proof balconies, so you can get close to nature without it getting too close to you. Tucked into a secluded corner of the famous Daintree, it is a sumptuous retreat in its own nook of wilderness, and its face-to-face-with-nature location means you don't have to go to much effort to experience the delights of the environment. No traipsing through jungles, no three-day hikes, no helicopter trips into the middle of nowhere. Even the walk around the lodge and down to dinner is a magical experience, with guests able to wander through award-winning gardens featuring ancient and rare vegetation, tropical and exotic fruits, a lily pond and a pristine waterfall before reaching the Bilngkumu Restaurant and meals that have a leaning towards gourmet bushtucker flavours. The Spa is similarly natural, and features all kinds of pampering treatments, including the 90-minute Walbul-Walbul body treatment, in which you are wrapped in mud as you recline on a magnificent carved timber 'wet bed'. Or you can simply indulge in a yoga or Ki session, laze by the small solar-heated pool, or walk rainforest trails. If you're feeling adventurous, you can elect to join members of the local Aboriginal Kuku tribe on a bush tucker and native medicine stroll, or take a four-wheel-drive day trip to modern-day Aboriginal communities. It is so gorgeous, that many A-list celebs have been known to sneak up here for some serious R&R and green tea before rejoining their glitz-filled lives.

The architecture is so extraordinary, the lodge has won multiple awards for 'green tourism', along with various other accolades from the likes of *Tatler* and other *Condé Nast* magazines. In a market that's full of supposedly 'eco-friendly' lodges and green retreats, the Daintree Eco Lodge & Spa is a place that takes both luxury and environmentalism to new heights.

Daintree Eco Lodge & Spa
20 Daintree Road, Daintree, Queensland, Australia

Phone +61 7 4098 6100

www.daintree-ecolodge.com.au

182

183

LANDSCAPE
Lush ancient rainforest

ARCHITECTURE/DESIGN
Tranquil cabins in the trees

BEST VIEW
From your balcony

Silky Oaks Lodge

It seems as if everything you see now associated with a spa-style getaway has the words 'healing' or 'retreat' in it. It's almost as if we will feel tempted to pick up the phone and book a flight just by hearing these evocative catchphrases. In fact, we often do. We can be so mesmerised by the pictures conjured up by such nouns and adjectives, we've usually planned the holiday – massage treatments and all – even before we've checked out the website.

The Silky Oaks Lodge and Healing Waters Spa has certainly pulled in the big descriptors: 'silky', 'oaks', 'lodge', 'healing', 'waters' and 'spa' are tempting enough on their own, but together they bring to mind a place where you leave your stress at the door and prepare yourself for a few days of sheer bliss. Fortunately, the reality of it is as good as the promise.

Located at the edge of the ancient beauty of the World Heritage-listed Daintree Rainforest National Park, in Far North Queensland, on the northern bank of the Mossman River, it is a place where architecture blends into nature. Accommodation is a cool mix of 'Treehouses' and 'Riverhouses', depending on whether you want to be close to the birds and breezes, or close to the soothing gurgle of the river, and each has been designed to blend serenely into

the environment, with barely a murmur of disagreement between the two. The Treehouses, which are dressed in natural timbers, have floor-to-ceiling glass doors opening to a wide verandah where a hammock awaits – most guests cherish the views, which take in the bustling life of the rainforest. The Riverhouses are more spacious, and feature oversized spa baths, also positioned to take in the forest vistas. To help guests unwind and forget the outside world completely, there are no televisions in the rooms; a telephone, CD player and Internet access are the only concessions to modern life.

It's easy to see why Silky Oaks hasn't bothered with too many electronic accoutrements – much of the entertainment here occurs outside, in the rainforest. There are several tours that explore the area, including the Daintree River, Cape Tribulation, and beyond, and guests can also go snorkelling and canoeing in the river, along with scuba diving off the reef at Port Douglas. It's a region rich with wildlife and spectacular scenery, from the Daintree down to the sea, and the serenity of the lodge makes you feel as though you're not intruding on the landscape, but rather gently experiencing it without making too much of an impact on the ecosystem.

185

Silky Oaks Lodge
Finlayvale Road, Mossman, Queensland, Australia

Phone + 61 2 8296 8010

www.silkyoakslodge.com.au

LANDSCAPE
Heart of the Daintree forest

ARCHITECTURE/DESIGN
Cool mix of tree and river houses

BEST VIEW
Atop your treehouse hideaway

COUNTRY

For some years now, New Zealand has become famous for its spectacular lodges, which are a curious mix of the kind of rough-hewn but strangely comforting rusticity you find in hunting lodges of the American West and alpine chalets. But recently, a new breed of lodge has emerged on the landscapes of the North and South Islands, and it's raising eyebrows with more than the locals.

Usually defined by a pristine location (often more spectacular than the lodge itself), a whisper-quiet atmosphere, a silent army of disarmingly down-to-earth staff and an extraordinary level of luxury, these lodges are setting a new standard for stylish getaways. These resorts may be top-drawer but they're certainly no fuss: even the high-style hideaways have a low-key elegance about them. The multi-award-winning Blanket Bay is one such example.

Situated just outside of Glenorchy, a small town at the northern head of Lake Wakatipu in the South Island, the region is so spectacular, Peter Jackson chose it as the location for the epic movie trilogy, *Lord of the Rings*. Think rugged high country, glacier-fed rivers and ancient beech forests. It is like nothing else on earth. Even Middle Earth. Although a tiny part of this majestic landscape, Blanket Bay Lodge seems to fit neatly into the dramatic scenery, it's as if it's always been there, even though the architecture is far from ancient.

The story of the lodge actually starts in 1969, when Pauline and Tom Tusher, a former president and CEO of the jeans company Levi Strauss, bought 22 hectares of secluded wilderness on a visit to the country. (The name 'Blanket Bay' evolved from the days when pioneer farmers sheared their sheep under rough shelters stitched together from blankets.) The Tushers, who wanted a place to retire to when they were ready to settle down, knew they wanted a retreat that was unlike anything else, but they were also determined to imbue the hideaway with a local flavour. They hired US architect-to-the-stars Jim McLaughlin to design the resort, and insisted on using materials native to the area, including woolshed planks and roof beams salvaged from old wharves and railroad bridges. Thanks to McLaughlin's talent and the Tushers' creativity, the effect was rustic, but far from rough. The stone-and-timber lodge, with its 30-foot-high Great Room, looks like it was carved cleanly out of the Southern Alps (as New Zealand's South Island mountains are known),

191

192

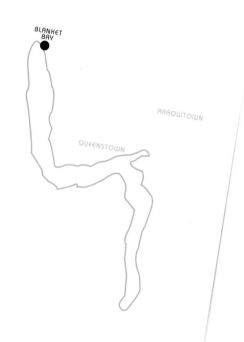

with their jagged mountain peaks and glassy lake drama reflected eloquently in the elegant lines and clean surfaces of the design. The interior spaces are also modelled on the scale of the landscape outside: everything seems oversized and thoroughly grand, from the Great Room to the 580-square-foot lodge rooms and the 700-square-foot lodge and chalet suites, with their stone fireplaces and sprawling 400-feet terraces. There are even steam rooms in the bathrooms. In contrast to the size of the spaces, and perhaps to soften them slightly, the Tushers made the décor simple: natural-fibre rugs, neutral colours, and baskets or wood tables for accent.

Such was the success of the final design that the Tushers eventually decided to open it up to outside guests, parlaying it from a private home to a bed and breakfast and then finally to the luxury lodge it is today. It was a natural choice: there is some of the country's best hiking and kayaking nearby, plus opportunities to go skiing, fishing for plump trout (some even elect to go

fly fishing, journeying down to the river by helicopter), picnicking or horse riding. (The lodge has its own stables.) There is even a 65,000-acre working sheep station next door, also owned by Tushers, which visitors can experience – usually on horseback.

In 2004, the UK *Sunday Times Travel Magazine* named the lodge the Ultimate Retreat while the influential magazine *Robb Report* placed Blanket Bay in its top 100 hotels worldwide in 2006. It has been so successful that the Tushers had to build their own accommodation next to the lodge, for the four months that the San Francisco-based couple is in New Zealand, just in case they couldn't get a room.

Everything about Blanket Bay is at once wild and cosseting, from the views of the lake to the cosy warmth of the roaring log fire; from the wild venison to the hearteningly good red wine. It is sophisticated but casual, and refined without calling too much attention to itself.

LANDSCAPE
Glacier-fed rivers and ancient forests

ARCHITECTURE/DESIGN
Luxe lodge meets alpine chalet

PACK
Walking shoes

Gaia Retreat

You would have to assume that a resort developed by the entertainer Olivia Newton-John was going to turn out to be tasteful and stylish. And indeed it is. In fact, Gaia Retreat at Byron Bay is much like the singer herself: a complete knockout.

Set up in the hinterland behind Byron Bay, where the hills provide a cool green escape from both the traffic of the town (especially during summer) and the heat of the beach, this new organic retreat is, like its owner: very Australian but with a touch of Hollywood glamour.

Gaia is the culmination of years of passion and plans formed by both Newton-John and her business partner and friend Gregg Cave. Newton-John has owned property near here for decades. It's understandable really, since Byron Bay has long been a place for people to renew their energy and restore their soul. Which is partly why Newton-John decided to develop a retreat here, not long after her mother passed away. She considers it her 'spiritual home' and now hopes others will feel the same way.

The difference between Gaia and other Byron Bay-based spas and health retreats is that this place fuses a palpable calm with an understated sophistication. The design of the various buildings, used for spa treatments as well as accommodation and dining, is subtle, so that all you notice are the lush gardens and meandering pathways. It's so sensitive that dozens of magazines and newspapers have included it in their 'Best of the Best' lists, including *Gourmet Traveller* and British *Vogue*.

For Newton-John, it is as much a retreat as a business venture. She still uses it for a pick-me-up between meetings and other commitments, sneaking in for a massage now and then. Other guests drift among the trees, indulging in the various treatments and bespoke programs, from yoga to creative classes. It's a hideaway for harried types who want to de-stress or detox without doing it too tough. With as much grace and beauty as its co-owner, it's no wonder Gaia achieved instant popularity from the moment it opened. As the song says: "Let me be there".

199

200

205

BYRON
BAY

BANGALOW

GAIA
RETREAT
●

LANDSCAPE
Byron Bay hinterland

ARCHITECTURE/DESIGN
Easy elegance with spa treatments on the side

PACK
Stress, because it's a good place to get
rid of it

Margaret River is renowned for hidden pleasures. There are the pleasures of the grape, from the hundreds of wineries dotted throughout the landscape; the pleasures of the sea, which can be experienced up close and personal via the plate or in the water; and the pleasures of the extraordinary scenery, which visitors like to take in by bike, convertible or just a good old family sedan with the boot piled high with wine.

And then there are the hidden pleasures of the various places to stay, which are so tucked away they virtually redefine the phrase 'secluded delight'.

The perfectly named Hidden Valley is one such retreat. Located in a pristine pocket of bushland deep in the heart of this celebrated wine and coast country, it is for those who like to be away from the crowds and traffic – well away. It is so private that guests say they can feel their cares drift away as they trundle down the driveway.

Designed to sit in harmony with the environment – the property includes a patch of protected forest and an abundance of rare and endangered animal and plant life – the retreat is spread into five distinct accommodation options, each of which makes a contemporary statement about innovative design. There are two eco lodges for those who like to be green; a stone stable for those with equine leanings; a wilderness cabin for those who really want to get back to nature; and a deepwater retreat on the edge of a secluded lake for those who just want luxury, privacy and modern design in one neat package.

Such was the fuss about this place, when it first opened in 2001, that it won all manner of accolades, including a National Tourism Award and an Australian Travel and Tourism Award. Part of the appeal of these five dignified hideaways was that they took edgy design and integrated it into the natural landscape in a way that represents a seamless merger of Mother Nature and man at his visionary best. The architectural highlights include an 11-metre covered timber bridge that links the main retreat of the Deepwater cabin to a luxurious spa cabana, plus a separate boardwalk leading to an island sundeck; glass-encased shower rooms with gloriously naked views of the forest; timber stepping stones leading to private outdoor spa huts; private entertaining decks with gas barbecues; and extended timber walkways and platforms with steamer chairs suspended amidst the forest – perfect for an afternoon siesta.

209

In addition, the cabins feature bamboo floors, fireplaces, cedar ceilings, and an intoxicating closeness to nature that makes you not want to leave your own hideaway. One cabin, the Deepwater Retreat, is so close to the lake that many guests like to plunge into the waters from the jetty provided. Others prefer to meander down to the enchantingly named Annie Brook for a spot of yoga or meditation, take a brisk walk among the rolling hills, or simply sit back and soak it all in.

It is a place designed to capture the spirit of the environment while creating a feeling of inner calm. Yes indeed, Hidden Valley was well named. The only trouble is, it is now so popular, one almost wishes it was a little more hidden.

BUSSELTON

HIDDEN
VALLEY
FOREST
RETREAT

MARGARET RIVER

LANDSCAPE
Margaret River's famous vineyards

ARCHITECTURE/DESIGN
Diverse, but distinctive

PACK
An empty car, because you'll be filling it with wine

Huka Lodge

Lake Taupo, New Zealand

Huka Lodge has a fascinating history. It was first established in the 1920s when a visionary fisherman, Alan Pye, decided he needed a simple fishing lodge to retire to after a day angling on the banks of the Waikato River, near Lake Taupo on New Zealand's North Island. He built the kind of retreat that could have been featured in a film – a rustic, simple, but utterly appealing lodge set in a dramatic, cinematic-style landscape of lush green hills with the Waikato River hurtling past on its way to the famed Huka Falls. The original building was barely more than a sophisticated lean-to, and contained Pye's bedroom, the kitchen and a large dining room that was full of atmosphere and the tales of anglers past. But the simplicity of the getaway, and the sheer beauty of its surrounds, soon attracted interest and fairly soon the reputation of the fishing lodge spread. Anglers far and wide came to fish in the Waikato River and then retire by the fire to swap stories with a whiskey in hand.

Many decades later, in 1984, word of this wilderness retreat reached present owner Alex van Heeren, who fell under its spell and decided that he had to have it. Injecting his passion and enthusiasm into the project, van Heeren expanded and embellished the lodge, without losing any of the rustic simplicity that

had so charmed previous guests, until Huka Lodge turned into the ultimate version of the great New Zealand getaway. While a majority of the guests still included humble fishermen and women, quite a few started to include royalty and Hollywood stars, among them Queen Beatrix of the Netherlands, Queen Elizabeth II and The Duke of Edinburgh, Lord Lichfield, Dame Kiri Te Kanawa, Sir Edmund Hillary, Bill Gates, Rupert Murdoch, Dick Cheney, Billy Connolly, Pink Floyd, Diana Ross, Robin Williams and Barbra Streisand, all of whom were either entranced by the landscape or hoped to hook the ultimate trophy trout. Alan Pye may still recognise the place – only just – but he would be blinking in surprise at the guest book.

Modelled loosely on the hunting lodges of America's west, complete with a great room, Huka Lodge owes its authenticity to the use of local materials. It is a lodge that looks like it has emerged naturally from the craggy landscape rather than having been erected insensitively upon it. It's almost as if landscape and lodge belong together.

The most striking architectural element about the lodge is the grand Lodge Room, a space in which you can imagine Robert Redford lounging by the

213

fire, tweed jacket on the wing chair and fishing rod by the door. Featuring panoramic views of the Waikato River and towards Huka Falls, the Lodge Room is the major focus of the resort, and guests frequent here day and night, drawn to the magnificent fire and pre-dinner drinks each evening. The library is also popular for a quiet read, and some guests love it so much they elect to dine here at night. The dining room is a study in country house romance, with tartan-upholstered dining chairs, chilli-red wing chairs, elegant black iron candlesticks and, of course, the requisite blazing fire. But there are also other places to dine if you want to embrace the view, including an outdoor terrace with open fireplace, or at a private table under the stars. Surprisingly, the lodge rooms are not the overly stuffed floral affairs you would expect of a country getaway, but have been designed in the same

unexpectedly elegant style as the rest of the lodge. In contract to the rich colours dominating the public areas, the colour palette in the rooms is muted coffees, chocolates and creams, but no less effective for it.

If inside is known for cosseting comfort, then outside, the lodge's grounds are known for their invigorating scenery. The lawns are so green, it almost looks like the colour has been painted on; the clipped cypress hedges lend mystique and myriad private spaces to sit and reflect.

Huka Lodge may have evolved from the humble fishing shack it once was into a sophisticated, slick international retreat, but its respect for the original mantra of appreciating the landscape and getting back to nature is still very much in evidence.

LANDSCAPE
Water-filled drama

ARCHITECTURE/DESIGN
Handsome hunting lodge

BEST VIEW
From a riverbank with a rod in hand

Lake House

There is something in the water at the Lake House. Quite literally. The hills around the villages of Daylesford and Hepburn Springs are famed for their natural mineral springs, and this hydrotherapy history has ensured that the region's picturesque getaways, such as the Lake House, have for years remained among the top rural havens in Victoria for stressed city professionals seeking country tranquillity. People come here to escape urban deadlines; to embrace the fresh air, and remember what peace feels like. They also come to indulge in therapy (of the best kind), with endless massages followed by copious amounts of fine wine and fresh produce. It is these last three that the Lake House serves up in ample quantities.

Set on the shores of Lake Daylesford, this personal, private and stylish boutique hotel blends the best of rural life with the sophisticated pleasures of fine dining and glamorous surroundings. It began as a restaurant in the French country style – actually it began as far less than that; when chef Alla Wolf-Tasker and husband Alan opened 20 years ago it was barely more than a horse paddock – and has since grown into one of the country's most highly awarded gourmet retreats. It is so renowned worldwide that it made it into *Condé Nast*

Traveler magazine's 2006 'Hot List'. Before the Lake House came along a few decades ago just about the only places you could eat in Daylesford were the village pub, the fish and chip shop or, if you were feeling fancy, the Chinese restaurant. Now, thanks to the ever-evolving Tasker and her increasing influence on other chefs in the region, you can indulge in freshly caught fish and just-plucked organic produce from local growers, all intertwined in lovingly crafted seasonal menus. (Autumn is the best time to dine here, with the season offering up much anticipated fare, from quinces to pumpkins, walnuts, game birds and other delicious meats and produce.) At the Lake House, you can even wash it down with a great drop from an extraordinary 10,000-bottle wine cellar – one of Australia's best. It says something when even discerning foodies from the city make the 90-minute trek to eat here.

But the food is not the only thing that sets the Lake House apart. The hotel's architecture is very different from the rest of the region's stone cottages and Italian-style villas built by the original Swiss-Italian settlers. Modern and luxurious, but still effortlessly comfortable, the poised white timber villas perched on the edge of the lake remain perennially chic through the seasons; pretty in summer, through the green canopy

219

Lake House
King Street, Daylesford, Victoria, Australia

Phone +61 3 5348 3329

www.lakehouse.com.au

of leaves, and striking in autumn and winter, when the bones of the landscape enhance the graceful beauty of their lines. Autumn here brings crisp, clear days and colourful landscapes awash with changing leaves from the European trees. Winter offers frosty mornings and mist-laden valleys: perfect for long walks before returning to the open fire. Indeed, a walk through the grounds and along the lake on such a day, following the swans as they drift over the ripples, is not only reviving but sets you up for dinner, putting you in the mood for more of the Lake House's aesthetic pleasures.

In a region famous for its hot springs, it was only a matter of time before the hotel had its own spa, the Salus Spa, which is set among the treetops and surrounded by waterfall-fed streams. This particular Lake House menu offers everything from hot mineral water 'geisha tubs' overlooking the lake to heated plunge pools, saunas and even tree-houses with hot-tubs.

Whether your preferred method of hydration is mineral water or something else, the Lake House has refreshments aplenty. The only problem is choosing what to do first. If only they could bottle the atmosphere as well.

LAKE
HOUSE
●

BALLARAT

MELBOURNE

LANDSCAPE
Lakefront

ARCHITECTURE/DESIGN
Lake-inspired sophistication

PACK
Your appetite, for the famous restaurant

Lilianfels

With a name that sounds like a sigh, Lilianfels is Sydney's answer to stress, pressure and the day-to-day hurdles of life in the Harbour City. Mention the name and people immediately lower their shoulders thinking of it. It just inspires that frame of mind.

This 85-room country house-style hotel, west from Sydney, is the epitome of the perfect country house-style hotel. There's the irresistible location, with the hotel set poetically against the dramatic backdrop of the famous canyons and cliffs of the Blue Mountains, two hours west of Sydney. There's the impressive architecture, which leans heavily on grand for inspiration. There's the cuisine, which vies with your grandmother's for home-made satisfaction. And lastly, there's the anticipation of the one thing you really come to the country for: peace. And Lilianfels has this last element in abundance.

In fact, such is Lilianfels' dedication to country house comfort that it's not surprising to learn the estate was actually once a real country house. Built in 1889, it was designed to be the homestead for Sir Frederick Darley, the sixth Chief Justice of New South Wales, and his family, and provided a home to the family for more than 114 years. The crisp mountain air was believed

to be curative for Sir Frederick's daughter, Lilian (thus the name), who was ill with tuberculosis. Sadly, she passed away at the age of twenty-two, but the estate continues to rejuvenate those who come.

More than a century after it was first built, it has been restored to its original splendour to cater for weary souls in search of fresh air and spirited living. Perennially awarded by Condé Nast *Traveller* for its spa and accommodation, it's now part of the prestigious Orient-Express Hotels group. And the Orient-Express touch shows through in every plumped cushion. Indeed, Lilianfels is so heartening in the way it has re-interpreted country house life for weary urbanites that as a guest it can be very easy to become accustomed to it all. There are the wonderfully enveloping, overstuffed sofas and wing chairs, the silver tea services that magically appear at just the right time of day and the views, which encompass a magnificent plunging valley in the mountains. The place has brought back into fashion a great many wonderful things that most of us had long since forgotten about – High Tea, for example, which drifts on into Cocktail Hour in such a seamless way that you barely want to move from your nook by the open fire, even for

227

an appetite-inducing walk. There are also the gardens, set in 2 acres of English-style grounds, which frame the estate beautifully, and come into their own in autumn, when the falling leaves make for a magical sight on misty mornings.

For those who need further pampering and rest, Lilianfel's Spa, which includes both indoor and outdoor pools, has become a renowned haven of relaxation – or you can just sink into your own extra-deep bath in your private room, and then wrap yourself in some of the fluffiest towels made and sink into crisp sheets for a good night's sleep.

But perhaps the best thing about Lilianfels and its clever interpretation of classic country traditions is the food. The hotel has not only made fresh produce and first-class cuisine a priority, but has also raised the standard of country fare to such an extent that it has become a gastronomic trailblazer among Australian resorts. It's ironic because outside the grounds it's mostly scones and cream territory, but inside Lilianfels the dishes are mostly organic, and all utterly innovative.

BATHURST

LILIANFELS

SYDNEY

WOLLONGONG

ARCHITECTURE/DESIGN
Country house luxury

STYLE
Cosseted comfort

BEST TIME TO VISIT
Autumn

At first, it may seem strange to come across a Mediterranean-style retreat in the middle of the Australian countryside. After all, cobbled courtyards, sun-baked terracotta-coloured walls and colonnades are more readily identified with the hill towns and cities of Italy than rural New South Wales. But then, driving through the sun-ripened vineyards of this famous wine-growing district, you begin to see the similarities: the Hunter Valley is perfectly scaled, with gently rolling hills and a certain symmetry in the way the vines are laid out across the region. Its residents are also passionate about wine, food, flavour and life, just like their Latin counterparts, while architecture, opera and design are just as big on the priority list as they are in Florence or Milan. In short, it's just like parts of Italy, and offers the same romance, only without the jetlag.

Reflecting the same finely detailed beauty and commitment to aesthetic standards as the rest of the area, the Tower Lodge is like a little slice of Tuscany in an otherwise classic Australian bushscape. Stencilled against the sky and outfitted in tones of ochre, it's concerned with form as much as function. Making a design statement here, it seems, is as important as choosing a

good wine. Outside, the building is a modern version of an Italian villa: all fierce lines and blocky geometry shaded in gentle tones of rich beige. Inside, it's more like a palatial Venetian penthouse, with grand mirrors, grander fireplaces, tapestry floor coverings and more candles than the Vatican. The colours are the most beautiful element of the Tower Lodge, and it's hard not to notice them when everything is in elegant shades of pistachio, nougat and latte.

The sheer daring continues through to the facilities, where a hot tub has been fashioned from a 1000-gallon oak wine barrel, while the outdoor area of the cellar door is a gravel-lined picture of charm. Pull up a high-backed Italian-style chair and uncork a red before you wander into dinner. Even the boardroom is a vignette of rural, Italian-inspired humour, with antique farm tools, including a scythe and spade, forming a quirky still life on the wall.

The Tower Lodge is not the sort of thing you expect when you venture out to the Australian countryside. It's just too daring. But then you realise it is utterly authentic, and for that reason alone it perfectly suits its unpretentious setting.

233

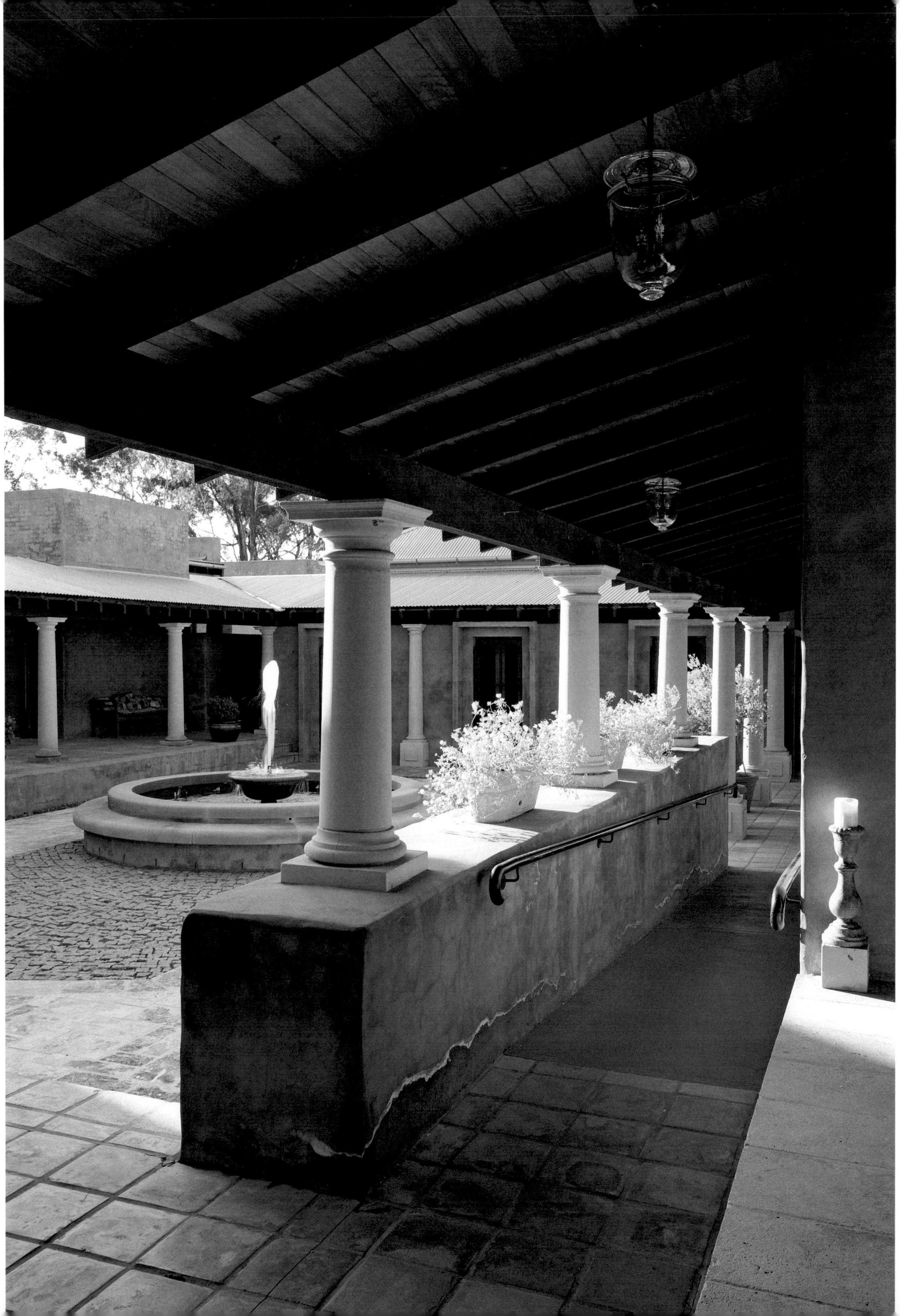

235

LANDSCAPE
Hunter Valley vineyards

ARCHITECTURE/DESIGN
Mediterranean-style minimalism with
luxe touches

BEST VIEW
On a road trip to go wine tasting

Tumbling Waters Retreat

Originally developed in the 1930s by a gentleman named Henry Halloran, who planned to build a palatial hotel on the site (it never went through to development stage), Tumbling Waters Retreat has been through various stages, from a Mecca for meditation (it was a favourite with hippies) to a healing centre, a top picnic spot, and then simply a great destination to generally gaze out and contemplate the view.

Then, just as the nearby Grand Pacific Drive and the new Sea Cliff Bridge started taking off in popularity, savvy sea changers Andrew Bergmann and Sonja Keller came and bought the land, perched on the Illawarra escarpment overlooking the bush, the Pacific Ocean and the hamlet of Stanwell Park, and set about building a multi-million-dollar sandstone retreat. The intention was to develop a getaway for stressed city professionals who wanted a quiet cross between a slick resort and private beach house. A clever vision if ever there was one.

Now, Tumbling Waters is a veritable oasis, tailor-made for stressed urbanites seeking a sea change, if only for the weekend.

There are only three one-bedroom suites and a separate sandstone cottage, but each overlooks the ocean and has enough extras to keep even the most jaded city slicker entertained for days. If the far-reaching sea views aren't enough, there are ample DVDs, plus binoculars (to view the passing whales and dolphins), Champagne, and of course a huge tub for two. There is also a steam room and hydrotherapy pool, for a detox and a dip. Even Mother Nature provides her own watery attractions, from myriad beaches to waterfalls, freshwater swimming holes and various restaurants featuring appealingly full wine lists.

The architecture of Tumbling Waters has been designed to sit in harmony with the surrounds, with private decks catching ocean views through a frame of gum trees, and rich colours reflecting the blues of the sea and sky. Andrew and Sonja selected the sandstone for the resort themselves from a quarry at Bundanoon. They also planned the stone bathhouse, which is built, rather cleverly, right on the edge of the escarpment overlooking the sea.

Surprisingly, they don't want to expand the place, preferring to keep it neat and intimate. It is a perfect example of the new breed of resort that aims to keep the experience 'personal', so that minds, bodies and souls are revitalized and restored, enabling guests to return to their urban lives feeling fully refuelled and oxygenated again.

241

LANDSCAPE
Coastal quiet

ARCHITECTURE/DESIGN
Water inspired

BEST VIEW
From the spectacular pool